SUPERMARINE SPITFIRE

Haynes

RESTORATION MANUAL

First published in February 2014

A catalogue record for this book is available from the British
Library

ISBN 978 0 85733 224 0

Library of Congress control no. 2013954657

Published by Haynes Publishing,
Sparkford, Yeovil,
Somerset BA22 7JJ, UK.
Tel: 01963 442030 Fax: 01963 440001
Int. tel: +44 1963 442030 Int. fax: +44 1963 440001
E-mail: sales@haynes.co.uk
Website: www.haynes.co.uk

Haynes North America Inc.,
861 Lawrence Drive, Newbury Park,
California 91320, USA.

Printed in Malaysia.

Acknowledgements

The authors would like to thank the following people for
their contributions and help when compiling this book:
Steve Vizard of Airframe Assemblies and Ian Ward of
VMI Engineering Ltd for their insight into restoring and
rebuilding fuselage and wings; Mark Harris and Andy
Nicklin of Supermarine Aero Engineering on what it takes
to machine and manufacture the aircraft components;
Peter and Stuart Watts of Retro Track and Air for their
account of the overhaul and restoration of aircraft
engines; Michael Barnett of Skycraft on what is required
to overhaul the propeller; Peter Monk of Biggin Hill
Heritage Hangar Ltd for passing on his experiences
of owning and restoring Spitfires; and Clive Denney of
Vintage Fabrics for his insight on painting the Spitfire.
Our gratitude to Timothy Burrows for a detailed
description of how to research the provenance of
your aircraft, an invaluable tool to the restorer, and to
Squadron Leader Ian Smith for taking us through the
process of an air test and sharing with us his enthusiasm
for the TE311 project. Also to OC RAF BBMF Squadron
Leader Duncan Mason for his thoughts on acquiring a
new member of the BBMF (Battle of Britain Memorial
Flight) fleet.
Thanks also to Keith Wilson and Andy Nicklin for
many of the photographs that appear in this book.
Finally, our appreciation to Jonathan Falconer and
Haynes Publishing for their patience as we worked on
this project.

SUPERMARINE SPITFIRE

RESTORATION MANUAL

An insight into building, restoring and returning Spitfires to the skies

PAUL AND LOUISE BLACKAH

Contents

OPPOSITE **A marriage made in heaven: Supermarine Spitfire and Rolls-Royce Merlin engine. The wartime development of airframe and engine went hand in hand to create what became – arguably – the finest piston-engine combat aircraft of all time. No wonder, then, more than 70 years later the Spitfire is the number one aircraft of choice for warbird restorers. This stunning photograph shows Spitfire Mark VCs of 2 Squadron, South African Air Force, in line astern formation over the Adriatic in 1943.**

Introduction

There is no mistaking the distinctive roar of the iconic Merlin engine on a still day as a Spitfire flies across the sky. The sight and sound is as much a draw today as it was over 70 years ago when people paused in their labours to watch as the nimble RAF fighter battled overhead against its German adversaries. There is still a great demand for the Spitfire to appear at events during the air show season, despite the current interest in new jet fighters.

OPPOSITE In the 21st century world of fast jets and even faster developments in aerospace technology, the immortal Spitfire remains top of the wish list for air show organisers and spectators. This is the Rolls-Royce Plc-operated PR19 (PS853) displaying with a Typhoon T1 of 11 Squadron. *(PRM Aviation)*

ABOVE Spitfire
Mark IAs from 610
Squadron, Biggin Hill,
during the Battle of
Britain.

The Spitfire's designer, R.J. Mitchell, died
in 1937 without realising how crucial his fighter
aircraft would become several years later in
the Battle of Britain. When production of the
Spitfire ceased in 1949, over 22,000 had been
built, with many being exported overseas
after the Second World War. The design of
the aircraft was such that improvements were
easily incorporated, both on paper and within
the production factories, leading to 24 marks of
Spitfire and 9 marks of Seafire.

Many regard the Spitfire as a British Second
World War aircraft that battled in English skies,
but it also saw action in the Mediterranean,
Pacific, South East Asia and, of course, across
the European theatre. The Spitfire served
as an interceptor, fighter-bomber, photo-
reconnaissance and trainer aircraft; some
even flew off the decks of aircraft carriers. Its
popularity around the world grew, from England
to Cyprus and Egypt, and on to India, covering
many countries and islands along the way.
The band of 'supporters' advanced from those

who had flown the aircraft, to those whom it
had protected and others who appreciated the
aircraft for its durability and design.

In June 1957 the last remaining RAF unit
flying the Spitfire, the Meteorological Flight
at Woodvale in Lancashire, converted to the
Mosquito and three of its PR19s were retired to
join the RAF's Historic Aircraft Flight (forerunner
of the RAF Battle of Britain Memorial Flight).
Even then it was becoming progressively more
difficult to see a flying Spitfire.

Today it seems unimaginable that the iconic
Spitfire should suddenly become surplus to
requirements, but in most cases post-war these
aircraft were simply scrapped or relegated
to the role of 'gate guardians' on RAF bases
across the country, where they stood at the
mercy of time and the elements. This was the
fate of many excess aircraft of the period, and
present-day aviation enthusiasts bemoan the
fact that there are (for example) only two flying
Lancasters remaining in the world. Modern-
day aircraft, when no longer required, are

ABOVE More Spitfire Mark Vs were built than any other variant of this fighter – some 6,487.

LEFT The Seafire F47 was powered by a 2,145hp Rolls-Royce Griffon 87 engine driving six-blade contra-rotating propellers – twice the power of the 1,030hp Merlin II or III that powered the Spitfire Mark I in the Battle of Britain.

often scrapped with no thought given to future generations being able to appreciate them in flight. Consider the ongoing struggle to keep the only flying Vulcan serviceable, as well as the long-term plan to restore the Lancaster bomber *Just Jane* to flying condition at her base at East Kirkby in Lincolnshire.

The Spitfire was an inspirational design and one that up-and-coming aircraft designers studied eagerly. This, coupled with the part played by the aircraft in the Second World War, has guaranteed R.J. Mitchell's brainchild a place in the history books and encouraged those interested in aircraft restoration to choose a Spitfire as their project.

In the late 1950s and early 1960s the appeal of the Spitfire as a private owner's aircraft began to increase and, with so few aircraft remaining in the air, the trend for restoring them began to 'take off'. Another event that fuelled enthusiasm for the Spitfire was the release of the epic film *Battle of Britain* in 1969, which featured several different marks of Spitfire gathered from around the world. Out of 27 original aircraft sourced for the film, only 12 were airworthy. Many of the present-day RAF BBMF Spitfires were used as 'actors' in the film, specifically PM631, AB910, P7350 (all of which featured in the flying scenes), and PS915, TE311 and MK356, which were used either for taxiing scenes or as static aircraft.

At that time restorers had many things on their side, not least the ease in acquiring an aircraft. For example, one that hadn't been fully dismantled could be languishing in a scrapyard; or the RAF may have been looking to replace a Spitfire that had served as a gate guard. Obviously, time is a significant factor in the restoration business. An aircraft used as a gate guard for perhaps 5 to 8 years will be in much better condition than one that has been left outside to face the elements for over 50 years.

Spare parts for the aircraft were also much easier to acquire, with many of the original factories still in business and carrying original spares in their stores. One of the most difficult

RIGHT Restoration
in the early
1980s, possibly at
Blackbushe. *(John
Elcombe)*

aspects of an ongoing restoration project nowadays is the sourcing/manufacturing of the parts required.

Another benefit for the early restorers was that the skills necessary for working on the aircraft, or for manufacturing spare parts, were still readily available. There are now very few people who have the experience to work on historic aircraft, in the servicing, restoring and manufacturing fields. There are no college or university courses that can teach the enthusiast and the only way to learn is to work alongside somebody who can pass on their expertise. Most of the original aero companies have long since ceased trading, but in their place are smaller, specialist companies that

RIGHT A wing stripped back to frame and ribs, again at Blackbushe. Note that no holding jigs are in use. *(John Elcombe)*

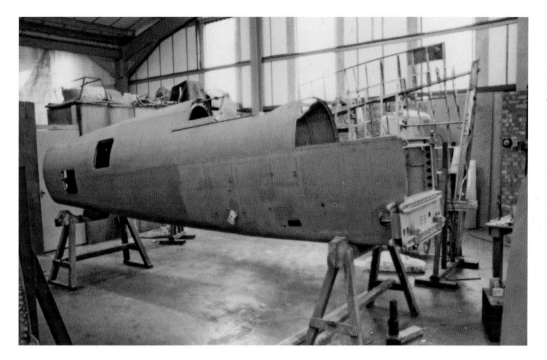

LEFT Fuselage in build; it is a late mark and Griffon powered, possibly a Mark XIV. *(John Elcombe)*

have emerged to fill the need of the modern-day restorers, in many cases their own passion for historic aircraft leading them to set up these businesses.

The interest in restoring Spitfires really took off in the 1980s with Charles Church who, along with Dick Melton, began such a project at Blackbushe in Hampshire. Unfortunately this partnership came to an end when Charles sadly lost his life flying in a Spitfire.

The next big step came in 1988 when Tim Routsis wanted to fly one of these aircraft. He managed to convince the MOD to remove Spitfires from RAF stations, where they were gate guards, and replace them with fibreglass replicas. He set up a company called Historic

LEFT A row of wings being restored, once more at Blackbushe, in the early 1980s. *(John Elcombe)*

Flying Ltd, based at Audley End, Essex, where these gate guards were brought back to flying condition. At that time Clive Denny and Ian Warren teamed up with Tim to carry out the restorations.

In 2001 Historic Flying was sold to Karel Bos of Bosel Exhausts and moved to Duxford, Cambridgeshire. Spitfire restoration work is still conducted there today, although no longer on gate guards, but on others that are in a much poorer condition. Such is the buoyant state of the industry today that several companies across Britain are involved in the restoration of Spitfires, with other similar companies in Europe, Australia and America.

Sourcing a Spitfire is difficult, but not impossible, and we will take a closer look at where to find a project later in the book. As in most things, money is the all-important factor. Not only in buying your aircraft, but also in

acquiring the experienced manpower to aid you in your quest and also in paying for the specialist companies you will need in order either to restore original parts or manufacture new ones.

Working to original drawings and specifications has proved invaluable to the restorer and over the last few years care has been taken to keep and store original workshop manuals and diagrams. To that end the RAF BBMF worked with Copyzone Ltd to digitise the original drawings for their historic aircraft and make them available on CD, thereby enabling easy access to diagrams, information and part numbers for those needing the information. The RAF Museum at Hendon has a catalogue of over 20,000 drawings that can be purchased for a nominal price per drawing.

In this book we take a look at the various companies involved in Spitfire restoration projects and examine in detail the processes necessary to identify when a part requires replacing with a new manufactured part, or when it can be restored.

The RAF BBMF has now completed its restoration project, a Spitfire Mark XVI (TE311). This aircraft proved invaluable in compiling the Haynes *Supermarine Spitfire Manual* (2007), and here we will be exploring some of the processes used in the restoration of this

aircraft's components and seeing how TE311 progressed to engine ground runs and, finally, to flight. At the end of the book is a list of useful addresses for some of the companies that offer specialist services to the restorer. (This book focuses on those companies that co-author Paul Blackah – as a restorer of the Messerschmitt Bf109G-2 ('Black 6') and the Spitfire Mark XVI (TE311) – has had experience of working with.)

ABOVE Spitfire Mark XIV, NH904, G-FIRE. This aircraft was painted gloss red by its owner, Spencer Flack, and was restored to flight in 1981. *(John Elcombe)*

LEFT TE311 on RAF Exhibition Flight duty. This came to an end in 1999 when she was delivered to RAF BBMF for spares recovery. *(RAF BBMF)*

RIGHT Spitfire Mark
XIV, TE311, pictured
at RAF Coningsby.
The fuselage has been
paint stripped so that
it can be assessed.
(Authors)

*Mark Harris, of Supermarine Aero Engineering
Ltd, gives his opinions on the trend for restoring
the Spitfire.*

The aircraft restoration movement concerned
with Second World War aircraft like the
Spitfire that we know today, began in Britain
in the late 1960s when the *Battle of Britain*
film was made. At that time it was possible
to source parts from military surplus dealers
and scrapyards. Historical accuracy was not
particularly important. With only a few flying
examples around the world no one got terribly
upset with a slightly strange mixture of parts
and specifications, or an owner throwing
away equipment or systems not required for
air shows or pleasure flying. As parts began
to wear out or were lost, local repair solutions
started to be used and each Spitfire adopted
its own unique specification, with a mixture of
types, modification states and varying degrees
of substitution of modern parts for old – in fact
anything to keep it flying!

Rebuilding or maintaining any Second World
War aircraft requires the procurement of many
component parts and assemblies, historically
much of this need has been satisfied by a surplus
of surviving spare parts or even donor aircraft.

Companies, organisations or private
individuals with an interest in rebuilding or
operating a Spitfire have to be, by necessity,
quite resourceful. They need a whole aircraft

skill set and typically employ the services of
ex-RAF, or big organisation-trained engineers
to 'get it flying again'. Engineers such as these
are generally divided into the following groups:
Systems, Power plant, Airframe or Electrical/
Avionics. Spitfire-specific expertise in any of the
above fields is rare; to be an expert in two or
more areas is of course harder still, but these
people must be found and kept if the world's
last remaining Spitfires are to be flown safely.

Flight safety should of course be paramount
in the minds of everyone involved in aeronautical
engineering; generally speaking, this is an
industry-wide philosophy and underpins
everything we all do. Aircraft can be safe,
practical and yet completely historically incorrect.

In restoring a Spitfire to a historically accurate
state, an often-heard remark is: 'It's like
doing a jigsaw puzzle with most of the pieces
missing and no picture on the box lid!' When
Vickers Supermarine stopped manufacturing
Spitfires no consideration was given to keeping
drawings, tooling or supporting documentation.
Naturally some information did survive, often in
seldom-visited archives of factories once busy
with the task of supplying vital parts to the vast
shadow factory network of production lines.
Most of this information has now been passed
on to the RAF Museum at Hendon where it is
being preserved with the reverence it deserves,
but sadly what survives represents only a tiny
percentage of what once existed.

So what is the attraction of restoring and, for those with a pilot's licence, subsequently flying those aircraft that have been brought back from (in some cases) something resembling a pile of scrap metal? The Commanding Officer, RAF BBMF, Squadron Leader Ian Smith, tells us of the excitement that he has felt while watching the restoration of Spitfire Mark XVI, TE311, slowly come to fruition, and the anticipation of the first air test, which took place a few months later.

Flying any Spitfire is special, although if you are fortunate enough to have a few to choose from there will always be a favourite. Rarely does one get the opportunity to air test a Spitfire as special as LF Mk VXIe. RAF BBMF, led by Chief Technician Paul Blackah, have rebuilt TE311 over the past decade to an airworthy condition. You only have to look at the pictures of her when she arrived on the Flight for 'spares recovery' and you realise the magnitude of their task. Having decided that she was worthy of rebuild rather than being stripped for spares the Flight has painstakingly returned her to an airworthy condition. Initially it was done in Paul's and Corporal Andy Bale's spare time, but for the past few years teams of engineers have worked on her to get her where she is today.

From an air test point of view she is no different to any other Spitfire the boys have prepared. I have ultimate faith in their professionalism and I know that if they say she is ready then she is ready. That said it is a special day. For Paul and Andy, and the rest of the team who have spent a decade and countless thousands of hours rebuilding her, seeing her airborne again is the fruits of all their labours. On a personal note I will delight in flying a new mark on the Flight and relish the fact that we are returning an eagle to her natural habitat 58 years after she last flew. Stuff of legends!

BELOW Back where she belongs: TE311, flying again after a painstaking 11-year restoration. *(Keith Wilson)*

Chapter One

Wartime Spitfire factory

During the Second World War it was essential to increase not only the productivity of the factories, but also to constantly improve the design of the aircraft to enhance its aeronautical prowess and improve its weapons capability. Factories were set up across the country and women, alongside men, played their part in building the Spitfire. For an aircraft designed and built in peacetime, it was to become one of the most recognised and greatest warplanes of all time.

OPPOSITE A Spitfire Mark I nears completion on the production line. Note the two-blade fixed pitch propeller. *(Mark Harris)*

Wartime construction of the Spitfire

In order to know how to restore your Spitfire it is useful to have some understanding of the initial design concept and history of the aircraft. The Spitfire proved a relatively easy design to adapt and improve and therefore had the capacity to evolve at a pace that mirrored the developments of the German fighters. The Spitfire's designer, R.J. Mitchell, was to die at an early age without seeing either the impact that his design had on the Second World War or the affection that a whole nation had for his aircraft. With the many marks of Spitfire, the restorer potentially, and subject to availability, has even more choices to make.

R.J. Mitchell

Reginald Joseph Mitchell was born in Staffordshire in 1895 with a determination and talent that saw him rise to Chief Engineer and Technical Director of Supermarine Aviation by the time he was 32.

Full of determination, he aspired to better himself after finishing an apprenticeship at Kerr Stuart & Co., a locomotive engineering company, and going on to be employed in the drawing office there. Working during the day and studying mathematics and engineering at night, he gained enough experience and qualifications to be employed by the Supermarine Aviation Works, based in Southampton, where he quickly rose through the ranks to gain position and more experience.

Although the Spitfire is recognised as being Mitchell's greatest achievement, between 1920 and 1936 he designed 24 aircraft in total, which also included bombers.

In September 1931 Supermarine had fantastic success with its S6B floatplane (S1595), which won the Schneider Trophy outright for Britain, an incredible coup for designer, company and England. Shortly afterwards the Air Ministry sent out a document specifying its needs for a fighter plane and setting out guidelines to follow. Mitchell received the document on 5 November 1931, read it with interest and determined that he could easily adapt his previous award-winning design to include all of the Ministry's guidelines.

RIGHT Spitfire people: R.J. Mitchell (seated centre) with 'Mutt' Summers (far left) who flew the prototype on its maiden flight, and Jeffrey Quill, Supermarine Chief Test Pilot (far right).

The following is a section taken from the guidelines, generalising their requirements:

Air Ministry's requirements for a single-seat day and night fighter
General requirements

a) The aircraft is to fulfil the duties of 'Single-Seat Fighter' for day and night flying. A satisfactory fighting view is essential and designers should consider the advantages offered in this respect by the low wing monoplane or pusher.

   The main requirements for the aircraft are
   i) Highest possible rate of climb
   ii) Highest possible speed at 15,000 feet
   iii) Fighting view
   iv) Capability of easy and rapid production in quantity
   v) Ease of maintenance.

b) The aircraft must have a good degree of positive stability about all axes in flight and trimming gear must be fitted so that the tailplane incidence can be adjusted in flight to ensure that the aircraft will fly horizontally at all speeds within the flying range, without requiring attention from the pilot.

c) When carrying the total load specified in paragraph 3, the aircraft must be fully controllable at all flying speeds, especially near the stall and during a steep dive, when there must be no tendency for the aircraft to 'hunt'.

d) The aircraft must have a high degree of manoeuvrability. It must answer all controls quickly and must not be tiring to fly. The control must be adequate to stop an incipient spin when the aircraft is stalled. An approved type of slot control, or other means, which will ensure adequate lateral control and stability, at and below stalling speed, is to be embodied.
The design of aileron control is to be such that operation of the ailerons in flight will produce the minimum of adverse yawing effect on the aircraft.

In paragraph 4 of the document it specifies 'Contract Performance':
The performance of the aircraft, as ascertained during the official type trials, when carrying the total load specified in paragraph 3 and with airscrew satisfying the requirement of paragraph 2e) shall be:

- Horizontal speed at 15,000ft not less than 195mph.
- Alighting speed not to exceed 60mph.
- Service ceiling not less than 28,000ft.
- Time to 15,000ft not more than 8½ minutes.
- The specified alighting speed must not be exceeded, but may be obtained by variable camber or equivalent devices provided that control and manoeuvrability are not adversely affected.

As can be seen by this brief example, the document, which consisted of numerous pages, was very specific in its demands. Despite this, Mitchell immediately recognised the potential that his original design held and set to work to alter his plans to incorporate the requirements of the Air Ministry.

ABOVE First of the many: the prototype Spitfire (K5054) on 11 May 1936, the day after its maiden flight from Eastleigh airfield near Southampton. *(Cambridge University Library)*

RIGHT This stirring wartime advertisement proclaims that the Spitfire is 'still the finest and fastest fighter in the world'.

Spitfire

Still the finest + fastest fighter in the World

VICKERS-ARMSTRONGS
LIMITED

It took him just 106 days before his design was delivered to the Air Ministry for consideration. As would be expected there were initial teething problems – the most worrying being that the armament system would freeze at high altitudes – and, for a while, the future of the Spitfire looked grim. However the engineers and designers worked tirelessly

and eventually this problem was solved by devising a system that would direct the hot air coming from the engines to keep the armament system from freezing up.

When it came to naming the aircraft, various suggestions were put forward, including that of Shrew, and it was some time before it was actually called Spitfire (an appellation that Mitchell himself thought ridiculous!). There are those who believe that the name was proposed by Sir Robert McLean, Chairman of Vickers (Aviation) Ltd, the parent company of Supermarine, whose nickname for his daughter was Spitfire. Whether this is correct or not, the Germans soon came to respect the aircraft that spat fire!

In May 1938 the first production Spitfire took to the air and in July deliveries began to be made to the RAF squadrons, with 19 Squadron, then based at Duxford, being the first active squadron to adopt the aircraft. By the start of the Second World War, in September 1939 there were 10 fighter squadrons using Spitfires with a total of 306 aircraft between them.

Over the course of the Spitfire and Seafire production the aircraft's weight increased from 5,280lb for the Mark I Spitfire to 10,300lb for the Seafire Mark 47 and its firepower was also

RIGHT A line of Mark Vbs with unpainted cowlings and fillet panels fitted. BL894 (third from the camera) went to 603 Squadron in March 1942 and was later converted to a Seafire Mark I. *(Cambridge University Library)*

increased from 8 x 303mm machine guns to 4 x 20ml cannons. Some marks could also carry 500lb bombs or up to 8 x 60lb rockets.

By the end of production in January 1949, over 22,000 Spitfires and Seafires had been manufactured across the various factories. The aircraft had played a major part in the Second World War, defending the country in a multitude of roles including fighter, reconnaissance and low-level fighter. Together with the Hurricane, the Spitfire and its brave young pilots fought through the Battle of Britain with a fortitude and tenacity that Mitchell could only have dreamed of, and it is unfortunate that he did not live long enough to appreciate the role that his design played in winning the war.

Spitfire factories

In order to increase productivity a number of other factories were set up across the country. Not only did they ensure a higher productivity level, but also guarded against enemy attack. Although the factories did come under attack on various occasion, they were not all targeted at once, ensuring that there was a constant flow of new aircraft ready to join the squadrons.

Supermarine Aviation Ltd, based at Southampton, was the factory where production began and was followed by three other purpose-built works across the country. The original factory was heavily bombed in 1940, which showed the immediate value of also building at other locations.

Castle Bromwich

In 1938, with the very real possibility of war on the horizon, the Air Ministry bought a site

adjacent to the Castle Bromwich aerodrome, Birmingham, and constructed a building for Spitfire manufacture. Installing machinery that was then the best technology had to offer, the factory employed local workers who were taught to use the sophisticated machinery; a purpose-built training room proved invaluable in instructing new staff and updating existing employees when improvements were made to the aircraft's design.

Although the government had been promised Spitfires by April 1940, the first aircraft rolled off the Castle Bromwich line in June and there were many problems – with management, staff and the reluctance to use Supermarine information in order to produce the aircraft that they had designed.

It fell to Lord Beaverbrook, the Minister of Aircraft Production, to bring about a change of management, encouraging Lord Nuffield to hand over control to the Ministry. Once this had happened Lord Beaverbrook was able to place an experienced Supermarine management team in the factory and give control over to Vickers-Armstrongs.

The factory operated on a 24-hour shift pattern and employed many women in engineering roles. At peak production the works employed 15,854 staff. By the time production ended the factory had produced 11,780 Spitfires, over half of all those built.

ABOVE Fuselage with frame 5 fitted. *(Mark Harris)*

LEFT Top and bottom fuel tanks in production. *(Cambridge University Library)*

RIGHT Fuselage requiring the skins to be put on. *(Mark Harris)*

BELOW A row of fin units being assembled. *(Mark Harris)*

Westland Aircraft Ltd

The Westland was already an established aircraft company, based in Yeovil. The firm had been producing aircraft for the RAF since the beginning of the Second World War and after the Supermarine factory in Southampton had been bombed it became a matter of urgency to find another one able to begin production of Spitfires as soon as possible.

The factory had four orders for Spitfires between August 1940 and March 1942, and from November 1942 until the last, dated March 1944, they had six orders for Seafires.

The ease in which Westland adapted to Spitfire and Seafire production was a great help to the government, who desperately needed to increase numbers of this aircraft that was proving so invaluable to the war effort.

ABOVE Frame 5 carry-through spars are clamped in a jig and the wing attachment bolt holes are reamed. *(Mark Harris)*

LEFT Wing nose ribs being attached to the spar web. *(Mark Harris)*

LEFT Wing rib 1 in its jig. *(Mark Harris)*

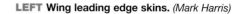

Cunliffe-Owen Aircraft Ltd

The Cunliffe-Owen factory, based in Southampton, was also already building aircraft and was easily adapted to produce Seafires for the Navy. They began production in January 1943, with their last order dated February 1944.

Southampton was in the unfortunate position of finding itself a prime target for bombing raids. With the docks bringing in supplies, and then the Spitfire factories, there was no better target for the German bombers.

Gordon Monger played an important role during the war years, working in the research and development department of one of the Spitfire factories. Adapting and improving the aircraft's design meant keeping the Spitfire's capabilities on a level with that of their German counterparts. Here, he recalls his time in the factory:

I got an apprenticeship with Supermarine and spent most of my time in the various experimental departments on Spitfires and Seafires, today it would be called research and development. Only short periods were spent in production which I found tiresome and monotonous after a while. Some people enjoyed it and became very skilled at doing one thing where they could work fast and make more money. Apprentices were on a fixed rate of about £1 per week. We worked long hours, no photography was permitted or mention of what we were doing. Also no talk of how many or type of aircraft produced. Subsequently I became a senior chartered aeronautical engineer working on various military and civil aircraft through the transonic era, finishing on Concorde and finally space.

It was on a freezing January morning in 1941 when I started work at 07:30 in the flight hangar at Worthy Down (HMS *Kestrel* near Winchester), where there was no toilet, no water, no heating and very little electricity. The work was very interesting and exciting. Here we modified aircraft, fitted different and improved engines including both the Merlin and Griffon. There were also

LEFT Fuselage in production. *(Mark Harris)*

LEFT Dispersed production at Wessex Garage in Salisbury where Spitfire fuselages are being assembled. *(Cambridge University Library)*

other items fitted to be flight-tested, as were all prototype Spitfire and Seafires brought, up to the point before the unit was moved to High Post on Salisbury Plain. Production aircraft from the Southampton area also came for their post test flight checks and correction of any faults. The production aircraft were then delivered to the various RAF units by young lady ATA pilots. Later I moved to the bottom hangar in Hursley Park (the Supermarine headquarters moved to Hursley House after being bombed out of Southampton) where the prototype Spitfires, Seafires and other prototype aircraft were built. After spending some time in the production machine shop in Short's Garage at Winchester I moved back to the experimental department and the drawing office.

When, and if, the changes and new aircraft and/or items were satisfactory, they were very quickly incorporated into production.

After being a part time student I spent two years at the post-graduate College of Aeronautics, Cranfield.

Dispersed production

I t didn't take long for the German Air Force to discover the location of the factories that were key to the aircraft production and to begin persistent targeting of them. With this in mind a cunning plan was devised to ensure the

continuing production of the aircraft in order to maintain the RAF's numbers.

Several small companies, such as garages and even a laundry, were identified as potential sub-sites, which were able to produce one or more of the components necessary to build a Spitfire, or perhaps assemble a smaller unit of the aircraft and in some cases even put together a whole aircraft.

These dispersed sites were grouped under various districts, which included Trowbridge, Newbury, Salisbury, Reading and Southampton.

LEFT Cockpit frames 6 to 9 and lower longerons being assembled by riveting in a jig. *(Cambridge University Library)*

ABOVE Frame 5 jig on the engine bearer mounts to ensure the correct angles so that the bearer will fit. *(Mark Harris)*

ABOVE RIGHT All major components were built on pre-formed jigs. Here is the jig for the radiator fairing. *(Mark Harris)*

RIGHT Nose rib 8 in its jig. *(Mark Harris)*

In each district there would be a manager placed in charge of the smaller units; for example, in Newbury the manager was Mr T. Barby and he supervised the following sub-sites:

Stradling's Garage	Detail fittings
Pass Garage	Process department
Nias	Tool maker and stores
Venture Bus Garage	Stores
Mill Lane Works	Sub-assemblies
Shaw Works	Press and machine shop
Hungerford Garage	Machine shop

There were 65 of these sub-sites spread over southern England, of which 46 were used for production and the rest were support units.

The airfields at Henley, Keevil, High Post and Chattis Hill were used for the final assembly and test flying of the aircraft.

ABOVE LEFT Frame 17 half completed in its former. (*Mark Harris*)

ABOVE Main spar attachment holes being drilled. (*Mark Harris*)

FAR LEFT Wing spar web being jig drilled. (*Mark Harris*)

BELOW Engine top cowling jig. (*Mark Harris*)

Engine development

To power the Spitfire a new engine was required. This became known as the Merlin and was produced by Rolls-Royce. The Merlin engine was first run in 1933 and completed its tests in July 1934. It was initially called the PV-12 (Private Venture – 12-cylinder) and was considered a major improvement on the Merlin's predecessor, the Kestrel.

The PV-12 generated 740hp and several more prototype engines had to be developed as there were so many snags such as coolant leaks and cylinder head cracking. The PV-12 evolved into the Merlin B, C, E, F and G as changes to the design developed. Eventually the Merlin F was deemed to be acceptable for the task required and it officially became the Merlin I. The Merlin G became the Merlin II.

The first Merlin I was fitted to a Fairey Battle, which was flown in 1936. The Merlin I was not a success and only 172 of this variant were made. The Merlins II and III were the first main production versions of the engine. The Merlin III had the universal prop shaft, which allowed the fitment of either Rotol or de Havilland propellers to be fitted, thus making it more adaptable.

The development of the Merlin continued and below are some of the characteristics of each engine variant that would have been fitted to a Spitfire.

Merlin II – First delivered in August 1937, used on the Spitfire Mark I. It produced 1,030hp using 6psi (pounds per square inch) boost at 3,000rpm.

Merlin III – Delivered in July 1938, used on the Spitfire Mark I. It attained the same power settings as the Merlin II. From late 1939, instead of using 87 Octane fuel, 100 Octane fuel was introduced and the engine then developed 1,310hp at 3,000rpm with +12 boost.

Merlin XII – This engine was delivered in September 1939 and was used on the Spitfire Mark II. It gave 1,150hp.

Merlin XX – This was first produced in July 1940 and delivered 1,480hp at 3,000rpm with boost pressure up to +14psi. This engine was fitted on the Spitfire Mark III prototype.

Merlin 32 – Production ran from June 1942 and this engine gave 1,645hp at 3,000rpm. It had cropped supercharger impellers for increased power at low altitude and was fitted to the Seafire Mark IIc and Spitfire PR Mark XIII.

BELOW One of many Merlins that have been meticulously overhauled by engine specialists Retro Track and Air at their premises in Gloucestershire. *(Retro Track and Air)*

Merlin 45 – First produced in January 1941, it delivered 1,515hp at 3,000rpm and had a maximum boost pressure of +16psi. The engine was used in the Spitfire Mark V, PR Mark IV, PR Mark VII, Seafire Mark Ib and Seafire Mark IIc.

Merlin 47 – This engine was delivered in December 1941 and provided 1,415hp at 3,000rpm. This was used in the Spitfire HF Mark VI.

Merlin 61 – Introduced from March 1941, it achieved 1,565hp at 3,000rpm at 12,250ft, and 1,390hp at 3,000rpm at 23,500ft. This engine was fitted with a two-speed, two-stage supercharger, which increased power at medium to high altitudes, and was used in the Spitfire F Mark IX and PR Mark XI.

Merlin 66 – This engine delivered 1,720hp at 5,790ft using +18psi boost. It was used in the Spitfire LF Mark VIII and LF Mark IX and was fitted with the Bendix-Stromberg anti-G carburettor.

Merlin 76/77 – Producing 1,233hp at 35,000ft, this was a high-altitude engine and was used in some later marks of Spitfire.

Merlin 266 – This engine had the same specifications as the Merlin 66, but was built under licence in America by Packard and fitted to the Spitfire Mark XVI.

The biggest challenge for the engine designers was to increase the power output of the engine, thus maximising the performance of the aircraft design. Initial problems included the lack of power generated by the supercharger and this continued through different variations of the engine design until Sir Stanley Hooker designed a more efficient supercharger, which gave more power. As time went on he combined two superchargers, in series, to rectify the problem of diminished power at high altitude. This was incorporated into the design of the Merlin 61. It increased the length of the aircraft by approximately 7in, as the airframe had to be altered slightly to accommodate a larger engine and therefore a larger engine bay.

Another weakness of early engines was that an engine would cut out if the aircraft inverted during flight. This issue was partially resolved

PACKARD MERLIN 266 SPECIFICATIONS

Packard Merlin. *(Retro Track and Air)*

Type	V12 cylinder, supercharged, liquid-cooled 60° piston engine.
Bore	5.4in.
Stroke	6in.
Displacement	1,647cu in (27 litres).
Length	87.7in.
Width	30.8in.
Height	40in.
Dry weight	1,640lb.

Major components

Valve gear	Overhead camshaft with four valves per cylinder, two exhausts and two intakes. Exhaust valves are Stellite coated and sodium filled.
Supercharger	Two-speed, two-stage with the boost pressure automatically linked to the throttle.
Fuel system	A twin-choke Rolls-Royce/SU carburettor with automatic mixture control.
Fuel type	100/130 octane.
Oil system	Dry sump with one pressure pump and two scavenge pumps.
Cooling system	70% water and 30% glycol mix.
Supercharger/ intercooler system	Entirely separate from the main cooling system, but is the same mixture.
Reduction gear	0.42:1.

in 1941 by fitting a diaphragm across the float chambers. This modification was named Miss Shilling's Orifice, named after Miss Tilly Shilling the designer, but it disappeared on later marks of Merlin engines by the fitment of the Stromberg-Bendix pressure carburettor.

GRIFFON 58 SPECIFICATIONS

Griffon engine. *(Retro Track and Air)*

Type	V12 cylinder, pressure-cooled, two-speed, single-stage charger.
Bore	6in.
Stroke	6.6in.
Displacement	2,239cu in (36.7 litres).
Dry weight	2,165lb.

Components

Supercharger	Two-speed single-stage supercharger rotor, diameter 13.8in.
Fuel system	Rolls-Royce fuel-injection pump.
Fuel type	Avgas 100LL.

The rear of the Griffon 58 engine showing the curved supercharger housing and control linkages. *(Authors)*

Griffon engines

The Griffon engine was initially developed by Rolls-Royce after the Fleet Air Arm requested an engine that had more power at low altitude, was more reliable and easy to service. The first prototypes, the Griffon I, ran in November 1939.

It was N.E. Rowe of the Air Ministry who first suggested trialling the engine in a Spitfire. Supermarine agreed to the initial testing and the engine was then redesigned in order to fit into the Spitfire airframe by moving many of the engine accessories, such as the CSU, to the rear of the engine. This engine design became known as the Griffon II and ran in June 1940. Work came to a halt, however, to concentrate on the smaller 27-litre Merlin engine. The Griffon was not seriously looked at again until the early 1940s. Unlike the Merlin, the Griffon was created to use a single-stage supercharger driven by a hydraulically operated gearbox. Early versions were mainly used by the Fleet Air Arm and were designed to give maximum power at low altitude. The later Griffons featured a two-stage supercharger and achieved their maximum power at low to medium altitudes.

Pilots who converted from Merlin Spitfires to Griffon Spitfires found that the aircraft would swing to the right on take-off rather than to the left, because the Griffon engine rotated in the opposite direction to the Merlin. This was more noticeable on the more potent later Griffon-powered Spitfires with five-bladed propellers.

The Griffon engine was eventually put into production and was fitted to several Spitfire and Seafire types. Listed below are the variants of the Griffon engine:

Griffon IIb – This engine delivered 1,490hp at 14,000ft and was fitted to the Spitfire Mark XII.

Griffon VI – Producing 1,850hp at 2,000ft, this engine was fitted to the Spitfire Mark XII and Seafires Mark XV and Mark XVII.

Griffon 61 – This engine gave 2,035hp at 7,000ft and also introduced the two-speed, two-stage supercharger with aftercooler, similar to a Merlin 61. It was fitted to the Spitfire Mark XIV and Spitfire Marks 21, 22, 23 and 24. Also fitted to the Seafire Marks 45, 46 and 47.

Griffon 62 – Similar to the Griffon 61, but with Rolls-Royce fuel-injection system fitted, this engine was used in the Spitfire Mark 21 and Seafire Mark 46.

Griffon 64 – This engine is comparable to the Griffon 61 and was fitted to the Spitfire Marks 21 and 22 and the Seafire Mark 46.

Griffon 65 – Like the Griffon 61, but with a different propeller reduction gear, this engine was fitted to the Spitfire Mark XIV, Mark XVIII and PR Mark XIX.

Griffon 66 – This engine is similar to the Griffon 65, but with a cabin blower-drive for pressurised aircraft, and was fitted to the Spitfire Mark XIV and PR Mark XIX.

There are many more variants of the Griffon engine. The last mark of Griffon engine used in a Spitfire was the Griffon 122, which incorporated a longer prop shaft for a left- and right-hand contra-rotating propeller. This was fitted to Spitfire Mark 21 and Seafire Marks 46 and 47.

MERLIN PRODUCTION TOTALS

Derby	32,377
Crewe	26,065
Glasgow	23,647
Manchester	30,428
Packard	55,523
Grand Total	168,040

GRIFFON PRODUCTION TOTALS

Derby and Crewe	8,108

(These totals are for all engines built, not necessarily fitted to Spitfires.)

It should be noted that with ongoing development of the engines, from the Spitfire Mark I to the Seafire Mark 47, the increase of power was approximately 100% and the top speed went from 350mph to 451mph, a gain of approximately 40%.

The Merlin and the Griffon engines were

BELOW The machine shop at the Rolls-Royce factory. *(Rolls-Royce)*

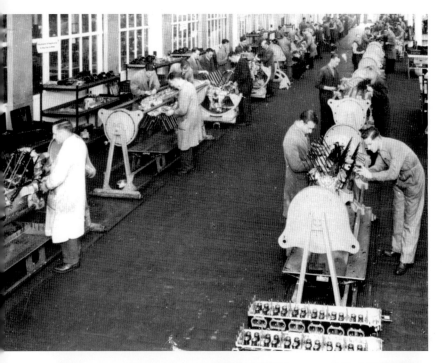

manufactured at four locations across the country, the idea being similar to that of the airframe factories: to have more than one site building engines in case of enemy attack. Ernest Hives, general manager of Rolls-Royce Derby, was the driving force behind the production of engines and worked with one thought in mind: to produce as many engines in as little time as possible, with the threat of war imminent. Once the war began he pushed for increased productivity in order to keep the flow of aircraft moving to replace those lost during action. The factories were as follows:

Derby

The Derby factory was located at Osmaston, and carried out the majority of the development work on the Merlin, with any flight testing necessary being done at RAF Hucknall. Derby also produced the Griffon engine.

Crewe

In May 1938 Rolls-Royce began work on a new works at Crewe, with production commencing in 1939. The factory was something of a bugbear to Hives, as initially he planned to man it with unskilled labourers, which eventually led to the employees striking as they felt they should be reclassified, and there was also an issue with the accommodation that the council had promised to build, but failed to deliver. Eventually difficulties were resolved and production began in earnest, manufacturing both the Merlin and Griffon engines.

Glasgow

With the bountiful availability of Scottish steel, Glasgow was the obvious choice as the site of an engine factory needing a constant supply of this material and so the factory at Hillington started construction in 1939, with production of engines beginning in November 1940.

With 16,000 employees, Hives encountered the same accommodation problems as at Crewe. This site was virtually self-sufficient, as

LEFT Pistons being machined. *(Rolls-Royce)*

all components were manufactured here, but it was a punishing work schedule, which took its toll on the employees. Stress-related illnesses began to lead to high levels of absences, so to tackle this it was decided to reduce working hours to *only* 82 hours per week with one half Sunday per month off.

Manchester

The factory at Manchester was based at Trafford Park, making use of an existing works on the site. It was opened in May 1941, and although staffing with skilled labour was a problem at the beginning, before long the factory was working so well that none of the engines produced was

rejected. As the design engineer Sir Stanley Hooker said, 'Merlins came out like shelling peas!'

As well as manufacturing engines in the UK, the Packard Motor Car Company began production in America, which helped greatly in increasing numbers. The first Packard Merlin was turned out in 1941.

Flight-testing

Each aircraft was tested on completion and prior to transporting to its unit. Criteria for air testing was developed and well-known test pilots Jeffrey Quill and Alex Henshaw led teams of test pilots at their respective factories.

Delivery to squadrons

Once the aircraft had been built at their respective factories their next destination was to the maintenance units to be fully armoured, and from there they needed to be conveyed to their squadrons. In a situation where there was progressively fewer experienced pilots on a daily basis, it was inconceivable to consider taking battle-weary, trained pilots away from their duties in order to transport these new aircraft.

After due consideration, the task was allotted to the Air Transport Auxiliary (ATA), a civilian unit formed in 1939 in order to move mail and supplies, and in the early days there were only 22 pilots. Commanding Officer Gerard d'Erlanger (formerly a director of British Airways) took charge of the unit, referring to the ATA as his 'Ancient and Tattered Airmen' in deference to the age and disabilities of some of the pilots.

The ATA finally gave women pilots the opportunity to fly on an equal footing with their male counterparts. Although women were not accepted in a combative role during the Second World War, there were many who were keen to be behind the stick of a Spitfire. After a nationwide appeal for volunteers, many women, who were fortunate enough to be qualified pilots, were interviewed and given posts within the ATA. They undertook another training course to assess abilities and to train them further on map reading, coping with the elements and flying single- and multi-engined aircraft. These women were then expected to fly any aircraft that fell into their specific category, often with no experience and just a copy of the pilot's notes tucked into their jackets. Many times astonished ground crew on a receiving station would watch as a lone woman exited from a heavy bomber and, when questioned as to the whereabouts of the crew, they would not believe that she alone had piloted the aircraft, and sometimes they would actually climb aboard to search for hidden crew members.

It should be remembered that these pilots, both men and women, were not trained in aerial combat and, in many cases, were flying aircraft that were without the benefit of radio and ammunition and were therefore at the mercy of attack from rogue enemy planes. Inclement weather conditions were responsible for numerous losses, most notable that of famous aviator Amy Johnson, who was lost over the Thames estuary.

Approximately 309,000 aircraft were delivered by the ATA, with losses recorded as 173 aircrew. In 2008, the surviving veterans of the ATA were invited to 10 Downing Street to receive a special Veteran's Badge in honour of their contribution during the Second World War.

Mary Ellis (née Wilkins) was one of the female pilots of the Air Transport Auxiliary, who delivered many different types of aircraft during her service. Among those were numerous Spitfires and here she recalls her first encounter with this aircraft, which obviously made a great impression and has remained a firm favourite ever since:

For as long as I can remember I have wanted to fly aeroplanes. Even as a schoolgirl it was my dream, and my loving, indulgent Father made this possible. I learned to fly in 1938; lessons were given in a B A Swallow and G Moth at Witney aerodrome. I managed to get my licence.

One day in 1941, quite by chance, I heard an appeal on the wireless for pilots that were required to join the ATA to be trained to fly aircraft from factories to airfields. I wrote immediately, back came an answer – to attend an interview at Hatfield airfield. I was overjoyed.

The interview went well, and I was invited to join the ATA, which I did a few weeks later. It was a huge step to take, being still a young girl.

The ATA training was very comprehensive and I soon became accustomed to a) flight with no aids (radio etc), b) battling with the elements and c) map reading etc.

After a number of single engine aircraft deliveries, including the Hurricane, I was at last given the Spitfire, in fact two Spitfires to ferry on 13 October 1942.

1) F/O Mary Wilkins Spitfire V AR513
                      South Marston to
                      Lyneham
2) F/O Mary Wilkins Spitfire V AR516
                      South Marston to Little
                      Rissington

Under the gaze of a disbelieving ground crew (I had said it was my first Spitfire) I climbed into the cockpit of their shiny number 5 Spitfire, AR513. After a study of the instrument panel etc, remembering the cockpit drill and with pilot notes tucked in my pocket, I started the engine. Awed by the throb of the Merlin engine, I felt the power coursing through the Spitfire and registering on the instruments. When okayed I taxied to the take-off point, weaving slowly along the track.

The take-off was just wonderful; the surge of power, which lifted us into the air was a great experience. The speed and easy controllability

was thrilling to me. This Spitfire, I found, was easy to fly and (mindful of my position in the ATA) with great joy I climbed and dived and played with a cloud, before setting on course to Lyneham. The Spitfire is a delight to fly, instant response to control stick demands, which needs only feather weight touch. It is the most desirable, beautiful aircraft ever to fly and also the most beautiful to be designed.

The Spitfire had its unique qualities requiring different operating techniques; the long nose required a different taxi operation, ie weaving from left to right. The nose was very heavy, so a man on the tail was the normal thing for taxying. The landing was different because of reduced forward visibility, compensating accordingly, I found this simple after a while.

In total I flew 400 Spitfires on ferry duty and only had two bad experiences. The first was a forced landing at Chattis Hill due to an undercarriage fault. The landing was a success, with little damage to aircraft and myself.

The second experience was when, in very thick haze, myself and my friend, both flying Spitfires, took off from Eastleigh airfield for Wroughton airfield. We somehow arrived over Wroughton at the same time, still in thick haze. We both landed at the same time BUT one at the end of the south runway and one at the north runway. We only saw each other as we passed on the runway. What a miracle!

LEFT Women of the Air Transport Auxiliary (ATA) delivered thousands of aircraft to the squadrons. This is Spitfire Mark IX, BS306, which the ATA ferried to 402 (Winnipeg Bear) Squadron RCAF on 26 August 1942.

Chapter Two

Sourcing a project

Once you've decided that the aircraft you want to restore is a Spitfire you'll need to source a project. In the 21st century this is a daunting task because complete Spitfires are becoming harder to find, so the restorer will have to be prepared to accept a project that may be severely damaged, incomplete or comprising just one or two large 'chunks' of Spitfire.

OPPOSITE (Main picture) This badly damaged but fairly complete Spitfire Mark IX is a typical project. **(Inset)** This wing section from a PR Mark IV, with some research, is also an example of a restoration project. *(Airframe Assemblies/Mark Harris)*

Why a Spitfire?

Why not? To be perfectly honest, the restoration project that an individual chooses is down to their own specific interests. Among aircraft enthusiasts you will find those who enjoy modern aircraft more than historic ones, and within the historic fraternity there will be those who prefer the fighters to the bombers; included in the fighter devotees are those who champion the Spitfire above the Hurricane, and vice versa. So the initial choice of project generally reflects a person's particular interests.

The Spitfire, with its classic lines and elliptical wings, is, for many, the definitive image of a fighter aircraft. It is the fighter that, as a child, many of us 'flew' in those furious imaginative dogfights across our back gardens, with friends following on behind with their models. As adults, some people will find themselves in a position finally to bring those childhood dreams to fruition; that Airfix model can now be scaled up to full size!

Apart from personal choice, another important consideration for the budding aircraft restorer is the availability of restoration projects. The Spitfire is one aircraft that has been relatively easy to source and restore over the last few years; however, it is becoming harder to find complete aircraft for projects now as demand exceeds availability.

A further concern when choosing which aircraft project to tackle is the access to manufacturers who are able to restore or repair parts of the aircraft or, where necessary, actually to manufacture new parts made to original specifications. Since the early 1980s there have been a small number of specialised companies in this field. The additional benefit of being able to acquire information from original manuals and drawings also makes a Spitfire restoration project a more attractive proposition.

Desirability

There is certainly an ascending scale of desirability within the aircraft fraternity. A Spitfire is highly desirable, but one that has seen active service during the Second World War has an added attraction. Then again, a Spitfire that has combat kills is even more covetable – and a Battle of Britain veteran Spitfire is a dream. However, the crème de la crème of all would be a Spitfire that has seen active service during the Second World War, with combat kills and that can be linked to a fighter ace. A fighter ace was a pilot who had five or more confirmed kills, so the greater the ace the more desirable the aircraft would be. Late mark Spitfires aren't as sought after as, for example, the Mark Is to the Mark IXs. Yet, it could be said that, at the end of the day a Spitfire is a Spitfire and is this attitude simply 'Spitfire snobbery'?

Condition and sourcing a project

With complete aircraft projects becoming harder to source – for instance the RAF gate guards that were removed and restored in the 1980s are no longer available – the potential restorer has to look further afield to find their project, perhaps even to a different country that operated Spitfires during and shortly after the Second World War.

Nations such as Russia, India, Burma and Australia still have Spitfires turning up, sometimes in the most obscure places; however, restorers are now recovering aircraft that have crashed and have been in the ground for decades, or even under water, such as Spitfire Mark I, P9374, which was retrieved from the sand flats off Calais. This type of restoration is now becoming the norm.

Museums with Spitfires on display are reluctant to part with them, even if the purpose would be to restore to flight. But if you had something to swap, for example a rarer aircraft that the museum would like, it may be possible to prise a Spitfire from them, especially if they had more than one example.

Once you have acquired your project and you are going to restore it to flying condition you should register it with the Civil Aviation Authority (CAA) in order to get a UK registration mark. If it is already registered, then you should still contact the CAA to change ownership just as you would with a car. A change of ownership should be done within 28 days of purchase. Any delay could mean that the aircraft is

THIS PAGE Spitfire Mark I, P9372, on display on the hangar wall at Biggin Hill. Given the state that it is in, if there are enough parts with data to prove provenance, this could be restored to fly. *(Paul Blackah)*

CONTROL COLUM
SPITFIRE P9372
P/O BILL WATLIN

SEAT FROM SPITFIRE
P9372.

RTLEY FLEW
MAY 24.
R DUNKIRK
T DOWN TW
P9372 WA
RAL TIM
CAN
TH

P9372

SPITFIRE MANUFACTURER DATA PLATE IDENTIFICATION

CBAF   Castle Bromwich Aircraft Factory
SMAF   Supermarine Aircraft Factory

BELOW Data plates are also a good source of information. This one, 39027 SHT14, is from a Mark XIX fuselage – 390 for Mark XIX, 27 indicating fuselage. *(Paul Blackah)*

BOTTOM This data plate gives the factory where the item was manufactured. SMAF indicates the Supermarine aircraft factory. *(Paul Blackah)*

Information like this on the oil tank is, again, invaluable and should be recorded before the tank is stripped. It gives the part number, mod (modification) state and the test pressure. *(Paul Blackah)*

removed from the UK register and, if already airworthy, that it would not be allowed to fly.

The UK registration number consists of five letters, the first of which is a G followed by a '–' and four more letters. Because you are restoring a warbird the original serial number of the aircraft is still allowed to be displayed on the side of the aircraft. The CAA registration code will also be featured, but discreetly, for example stamped on a metal plate that is located on the inside of the radio hatch.

To apply for registration you need to fill in a CA1 application form along with a nominal fee to complete registration.

Provenance, mark of Spitfire

Depending on how complete your project is, will determine how easy it is to find the provenance of the aircraft. The Spitfire has various data plates positioned on the airframe, namely one on frame 5 and one under, or around, the datum longeron in the cockpit to the starboard side. This plate will have a factory serial number on it, for example CBAF 1234. The CBAF stands for Castle Bromwich Aircraft Factory; the digits indicate the number off the production line. It will also have the part number of the item, which should enable you to establish the mark of the aircraft.

From the information on the manufacturer's data plate, and using various sources – such as books (see appendices) and the RAF Air Historical Branch, where they keep the Air Movement Card (AM Form 78) – it is possible to establish the serial number and therefore the history/provenance of your aircraft. The AM Form 78 tells you all the units that your aircraft served with along with any repair work that may have been carried out. Using the Aircraft Accident Record, AM 1180, you can then find out whether your aircraft had any accident, which may have led to the logged repairs.

The AM 78 and AM 1180 forms can be a little bit confusing if you don't understand what all the abbreviations stand for. The following gives a list of commonly used abbreviations along with a list of the damage categories.

43 Grp D/A	43 Group Deposit Account – a list of aircraft awaiting or undergoing repair or modification.
AACU	Anti-aircraft Co-operation Unit
AAP	Aircraft Acceptance Park
A/C	Aircraft
ACU	Aircraft Delivery Unit
AEF	Air Experience Flight
AFS	Advanced Flying School
AGS	Air Gunnery School
AGT	Airwork and General Trading – a firm undertaking work as part of the Civilian Repair Organisation
ANS	Air Navigation School
ASS	Air Signal School
AST	Air Service Training
ASU	Aircraft Storage Unit
ATFERO	Atlantic Ferry Organisation
AW/CN	Awaiting Collection
BATF	Beam/Blind Approach Training Flight
BCBS	Bomber Command Bombing School
BDTF	Bomber Defence Training Flight
BFTS	Basic Flying Training School
BGS	Bombing and Gunnery School
CF	Communications Flight/Conversion Flight
CFS	Central Flying School
CGS	Central Gliding School/Central Gunnery School
(C)OTU	(Coastal) Operational Training Unit
CRO	Civilian Repair Organisation
CRP	Contractors Repair Party
CS(A)	Controller of Supply (Aircraft)
DBF	Destroyed By Fire
DBR	Damaged Beyond Repair
EAAS	Empire Air Armament School
ECFS	Empire Central Flying School
E/F	Engine Failure
EFTS	Elementary Flying Training School
E&RFTS	Elementary and Reserve Flying Training School
FA	Flying Accident
FB	Flying Battle
FBSU	Flying Boat Service Unit
FEAF	Far East Air Force
FIS	Fighter Instructor School
F/L	Forced Landing
FRU	Fleet Requirements Unit
FTFlt	Ferry Training Flight
FTS	Ferry Training School
FTU	Ferry Training Unit
GAL	General Aircraft Ltd – part of the CRO
GR	General Reconnaissance
GSU	Group or Ground Support Unit
HGCU	Heavy Glider Conversion Unit
HSU	Heavy Conversion Unit
HTCU	Heavy Transport Conversion Unit
IFTS	Initial Flying Training School
MCU	Meteorological Conversion Unit

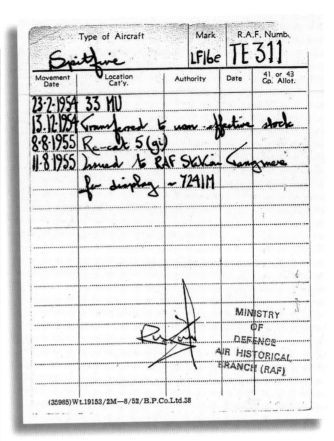

ABOVE The Form 78 gives TE311's movements from 1954 to 1955 when the aircraft became a gate guardian at RAF Tangmere.

MEAF	Middle East Air Force
MSFU	Merchant Ship Fighter Unit
MU	Maintenance Unit
NEA	Non-Effective Aircraft
OADF/U	Overseas Aircraft Delivery Flight/Unit
(O)AFU	(Observer) Advanced Flying Unit
OCU	Operational Conversion Unit
OTU	Operational Training Unit
(P)AFU	(Pilot) Advanced Flying Unit
PATP	Packed Aircraft Transit Pool
RAAA	Repaired And Awaiting Allocation
RFS	Reserve Flying School
RIW	Repaired In Works
ROS	Repaired On Site
RS	Radio School
RSU	Repair and Salvage Unit
SFTS	Service Flying Training School
SOC	Struck Off Charge
SoTT	School of Technical Training
Sqd	Squadron
Sqn	Squadron
UAS	University Air Squadron
U/S	Unserviceable
VGS	Volunteer Gliding School
WFU	Withdrawn From Use
WS	Wireless School

DAMAGE CATEGORIES

Before 1941

Cat. U	Undamaged
Cat. M(u)	Capable of being repaired on site by the operating unit
Cat. M(c)	Beyond the unit's capacity to repair
Cat. R(B)	Repair on site is not possible, the aircraft must be dismantled and sent to a repair facility
Cat. W	Write-off

1941–52

Cat. U	Undamaged
Cat. A	Aircraft can be repaired on site
Cat. Ac	Repair is beyond the unit's capacity, but can be repaired on site by another unit or contractor
Cat. B	Beyond repair on site, but repairable at a maintenance unit or contractor's works
Cat. C	Allocated to instructional airframe duties (for ground training)
Cat. E	Write-off
Cat. E1	Write-off, but considered suitable for component recovery
Cat. E2	Write-off and only suitable for scrap
Cat. E3	Burnt out
Cat. Em	Missing from an operational sortie. (Missing aircraft were categorised Em after 28 days missing)

1952–61

Cat. 1	Undamaged and can remain in service
Cat. 2	Aircraft can be repaired within the second-line servicing capability of the parent or nearest unit
Cat. 3	The repair is beyond the capabilities of the parent or nearest unit and will be carried out as indicated by the following suffixes:
Cat. 3 (Rep) C	The aircraft is repairable on site by a contractor's working party
Cat. 3 (Rep) S	The aircraft is repairable on site by a suitably qualified service unit
Cat. 3 (Rep) C fly	The aircraft can be flown to the contractor's works after temporary repair, if necessary under restricted flight conditions
Cat. 3 (Rep) C deferred	The aircraft may be flown under limiting conditions specified by the holding unit until a suitable repair date is agreed with the controlling authority
Cat. 4 (Rep)	Not repairable on site, because special facilities and/or equipment is required. Aircraft in this category will be repaired at a contractor's works after temporary repair, if necessary under restricted flight conditions
Cat. 4 (Rogue)	The parent unit and/or the controlling authority have conducted technical investigations and air tests and have concluded that the aircraft has unsatisfactory flying characteristics.
Cat. 5(c)	Beyond economical repair or surplus, but is recoverable for breakdown to components, spares and scrap
Cat. 5(s)	Beyond economical repair or surplus and only fit for disposal as scrap
Cat. 5(gi)	Beyond economical repair or surplus, but suitable for ground instructional use
Cat. 5(m)	Missing

Revealing the past

Timothy Burrows, formerly an engine technician at RAF BBMF, was instrumental in researching the history of Spitfire Mark LF XVIe, TE311, and he explains how he set about the task and his end results:

My brief direct association with Spitfire TE311 began with her arrival, by road transport, along with TB382 at the RAF BBMF, based at RAF Coningsby, during the 1999 winter maintenance season, where I was serving as a Junior Technician with the propulsion team. The priority at the time was the potential spares recovery opportunities these two airframes represented, rather than their history or any likelihood that they could ever fly again. There was speculation that they may be struck off charge altogether and put up for auction, now their use as exhibition aircraft had come to an end. Thankfully though, by the time I was posted away from the Flight in the latter half of 2002, the outlook for these two airframes had become more secure in the custody of the BBMF and I, along with other members of

the ground crew team, had already removed a number of components for refurbishment, so they could be put to good use in keeping the other aircraft of the Flight in the air. From a propulsion trade point of view the spares opportunities had been fairly fruitful; both aircraft still possessed fairly complete Packard Merlin 266 engines, although many of the ancillaries such as cooling and oil pipes etc were missing, and the radiators and coolers that had not already been previously salvaged in years past looked like they may be beyond repair due to the ravages of time.

Summer of 2004 brought me back to RAF Coningsby as part of the Eurofighter team. This gave me an opportunity to reacquaint myself with friends on the Flight, particularly Chief Technician Paul Blackah who, with the help of a couple of other enthusiastic volunteers, had decided to take on the gradual restoration of TE311's fuselage to a potentially airworthy state. Despite years of being regularly assembled and disassembled by the staff of the RAF Exhibition Flight, Paul and his volunteers had found her to be in reasonably good

ABOVE RAF Form 1180 Accident Report gives information on TE311's incident at RAF Aston Down in 1951: who was flying the aircraft, where the accident took place and what happened, the aircraft's flying hours and what category of damage has occurred.

condition and an asset worth saving in her own right. Sadly, TB382 had suffered from extensive structural corrosion, and was therefore only suitable for total spares recovery. The fact that Paul was now undertaking this restoration reawakened an interest in establishing the true history of the aircraft. Frustratingly, none of her records or flight servicing documentation Form 700 appeared to have been retained by the RAF and what little information we did have, came from the book *Spitfire, The History* written by Eric Morgan and Edward Shacklady (1987). This publication, at the time, was taken to be the most definitive information available on the Spitfire and in particular individual aircraft histories. Therefore, encouraged by Paul, I started on a journey of discovery, which eventually culminated in a visit to The National Archives at Kew in 2006.

The journey really began in 2005 and, to begin with, the internet became my initial and primary research tool, as it was easily accessible from the comfort of home, particularly after a long day 'at the office'. Using the internet in this way was at the time, for me, a new experience and I was pleasantly surprised to find that information in regard to the history of Spitfire TE311 was indeed available on the web. These early internet searches, however, provided two differing historical accounts for the aircraft, one of which, unsurprisingly, supported the work of Morgan and Shacklady. I presumed at the time that the authors of these internet articles may have read the book. The Morgan and Shacklady entry suggested that TE311 had spent time with 6 OTU, which they stated was later renamed 236 OCU, and 631 Squadron, again subject to renaming as 20 Squadron, with the date of December 1947 attached to this entry; the date the squadrons merged perhaps or when the aircraft joined the squadron? They also made mention of the aircraft taking part in the 1960s film *Battle of Britain* and at the time of the book's writing, the location of TE311 was given as RAF Abingdon, with the maintenance number of 7241M, although they further included the number 7741M but in brackets (note: maintenance numbers are generally issued when aircraft are finally withdrawn from flying duties and used for ground-based

activities such as training). So how to prove this account factual; had these units, for example, operated Spitfires and in particular the Mark XVI (and hopefully this aircraft)? Did 631 Squadron become 20 Squadron and was this in late 1947? Did the aircraft have a part in the *Battle of Britain* film in the 1960s? (This initially seemed implausible, given the fact TE311 was a late low-back model with the teardrop canopy, a characteristic out of keeping with the early model Spitfires in service in the summer of 1940, although a number of internet articles did suggest her involvement in the film). Finally, why the two maintenance numbers?

Another publication on the market at the time, which could possibly help prove or disprove some of the above claims, was *RAF Squadrons*, by Wing Commander C.G. Jefford MBE, RAF (1988). This publication was being marketed as the most authoritative work on the history of all RAF squadrons to its date of printing, so appeared to be a good place as any to start looking into the histories of both 631 and 20 Squadrons; unfortunately units such as OTUs and OCUs were not covered. Interestingly, both squadrons had operated the Mark XVI Spitfire (a good start); however, 20 Squadron had disbanded in 1947 while operating Hawker Tempests, not reappearing again until the renaming of the Spitfire XVI (and Martinet) equipped 631 Squadron in 1949 (Jefford, 1988). Useful information, but not really conclusive and no evidence that TE311 was ever one of 631's allocation of Spitfires.

By chance, in early 2005, I was invited on a BBMF trip to the RAF Museum at Hendon. While there, we were introduced to a number of staff responsible for the archive of documents held within the museum. I took the opportunity to enquire if they could help find out more about the circumstances of the loss of my Uncle, who served as a Wireless Operator/Air Gunner, in April 1945. Unfortunately they were unable to help, however they did enlighten me to the fact that many of the Aircraft Movement Cards (AM Form 78) for aircraft long since lost (destroyed) or retired from service, were still held with the Air Historical Branch (RAF) at the Ministry of Defence.

In late 2005 I wrote to the branch in the hope that they held the Form 78 for TE311.

Their response was swift and positive and, within two weeks, I had a copy of not only the requested movement card, but also a copy of an Aircraft Accident Record card (AM Form 1180). This was the first tangible evidence that supported the 'alternative' aircraft history as previously found on the internet, to that given by Morgan and Shacklady (1987). The additional information from the Form 1180 indicated the aircraft had been involved in a landing accident in June 1951, while serving with 1689 Ferry Pilot Training Flight at RAF Aston Down. The aircraft's presence at Aston Down and subsequent accident was also recorded on the movement card, an added bonus as the two documents cross-referenced each other, or at least in part. The Form 1180 also provided a number of additional interesting facts including the date, time and type of sortie being undertaken, the name and rank of the pilot (Flt Lt Doig, R.M., of South Africa), plus the total flying hours accrued by the pilot and a brief account of the accident itself (tyre burst on landing). One aspect of the account on the two documents, however,

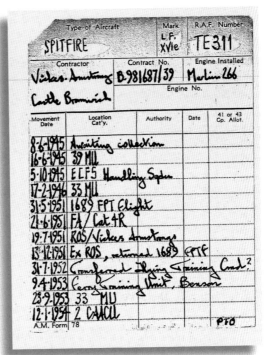

LEFT AND BELOW
The reverse of the Form 1180 (below) contains further information about what happened to TE311. The Form 78 (left) lists the aircraft's movement history and tells us that TE311 was repaired on site (ROS) by a work party from Vickers-Armstrongs.

did not match; on the movement card TE311 is described on the day of the flying accident as 'FA/Cat 4R' (damage category), whereas the accident record states under a column heading of 'DAMAGE' 3/3. Having found on

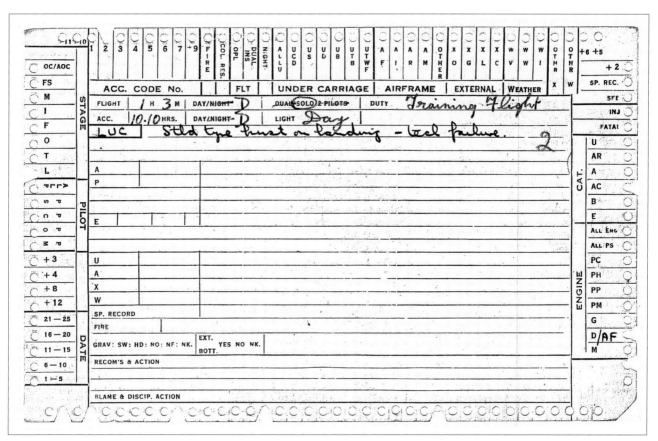

the RAF Museum website a document listing abbreviations for both these forms, a damage category of 3/3 did not appear to exist, at least according to the museum. (The significance of 3/3 is still unknown.) With regard to Cat. 4R, this could possibly either refer to Cat. 4 (Rep), which indicates the aircraft is not repairable on site and would need taking to a contractor's works, or Cat. 4 (Rogue), but this refers to aircraft with unsatisfactory flying characteristics. However, neither of these fit with the next entry on the card, which stated that TE311 was 'ROS/Vickers Armstrong', as ROS supposedly indicates 'Repaired On Site'. An on-site repair by a contractor would, according to the list, be Cat. 3 (Rep) C. Adding further to the confusion (and mystery) was the museum's assertion that these types of category were not introduced by the RAF until the following year of 1952. Therefore a repair on site by a contractor would, in 1951, have been a Cat. Ac (according to the museum list again). However, the Form 1180 has more to it and can take a little understanding as there are a number of additional headings around the edge of the form (on both sides), with a series of lettered or numbered codes allotted to each heading. One of these is 'CAT.' (obvious really) and there is AC marked not with pen, but a section cut out of the edge of the form. Closer inspection of this photocopy of the original form shows more codes marked in this way.

The 'alternative' history as given by the movement card (and in part supported by the accident record), suggested that TE311 had not in actual fact served with any operational squadron within the Royal Air Force, but had spent much of her time after leaving the Castle Bromwich aircraft factory in June 1945, either in storage (primarily with 33 Maintenance Unit) or involved in training ferry pilots at RAF Aston Down and later RAF Benson, with a brief initial spell with the Empire Central Flying School (ECFS) at RAF Hullavington, attached to their Handling Squadron. About the only piece of information on the movement card which corresponded to the book, was the issue in 1955 of the maintenance number 7241M (no mention though of the other number, which is still unresolved).

The photocopy of the FM 78 was of little

concern, as on closer scrutiny most of the information on the card appeared to have been entered and recorded by one hand. This suggested that the card held could be in itself a copy of an original. Also, other key information such as type, mark and number of the aircraft had been erased with liquid paper correcting fluid and re-entered with TE311's details. Therefore I felt justified in again questioning the accuracy even of this documentation, although the accident record card did give me some confidence that I may now have the true early history of the aircraft.

Another form of evidence which also supported the potential suitability for ferry training was the aircraft itself, as it was clear from the remaining fixtures and fittings that there was provision for additional rear fuel tanks within the fuselage and the installation of a 90 gallon external 'slipper' tank (the release 'tipping' brackets associated with the 90 gallon external tank were still on the underside of the inner rear wings), indicating that TE311 had been built with long range operations in mind. Examining the aircraft further also highlighted another unusual, but non-standard feature on the airframe, that of a series of small holes drilled into the sides of the upper rear fuselage. These, as it turned out, supported the fact TE311 had indeed taken part in the *Battle of Britain* film, but as a ground use airframe (possibly being restored to taxiing condition). To overcome the low back profile issue, a false high back had been fitted by the film makers. Corroboration of this came in early 2006 with the discovery of a photo of TE311 (finished in silver) undergoing the 'conversion'; Paul I believe found this key piece of evidence from a European sourced historical account of the film making and aircraft involved.

Other photographic evidence coming to light through further internet research, placed the aircraft on gate guardian duties at RAF Benson in 1971 (a station TE311 had operated from in 1953 according to the movement card) and at various locations during her time with the Exhibition Flight, including one at Duxford in 1998 masquerading as MK178 (this I could confirm as I was there at the time). The silver finish shown in the 'conversion' photo also supported information from another internet site, which had published an account of the aircraft's history. The majority of the transcript was credited by the site author to Gordon Riley and Graham Trant, from their book *Spitfire Survivors Round the World*, which suggested the aircraft had been on the gate at RAF Tangmere in this silver finish prior to being loaned to Spitfire Productions Ltd for the film. The article highlighted the possibility that Riley and Trant had also read the Form 78, as the aircraft movements they listed were almost copied word for word as given on the card. However, there was no mention of any of the additional information given on the accident record form.

With the information on the movement card potentially being the true history, I now embarked on trying to gather any evidence of the aircraft's actual presence at the locations given. As the aircraft apparently had two stays at RAF Benson, I enquired if they still held any information or photographs in respect of TE311, but although initial enquiries sounded positive, nothing eventually came from this line of investigation. An article published on the Royal Air Force's own website into the history of RAF Lyneham, gave an interesting insight into the activities of 33 Maintenance Unit (MU). The text suggested that in late 1946 the MU were holding at the station some 750 aircraft, most of which were Spitfires and apparently some of these aircraft were stored in hangars tipped on to their noses, while others braved the elements outside. Considering TE311 was supposedly there during this time, makes you wonder how she survived to be brought back into use four years later. Information on Aston Down and 1689 FPTF with regard to TE311 has proved elusive and inconclusive in actually placing TE311 at these locations.

An information sheet, provided again by the RAF Museum, on the types of documents used by the RAF, indicated that particular unit or station records of a historical nature were stored at the Public Records Office (or The National Archives) based at Kew under AIR 27. The Archive's own website allowed you to search for documents held in this section, although to view contents had to be done in person. Therefore, I started looking for any references to the locations given on the movement card, after

drawing a blank with inputting TE311 into their search engine. Thankfully, searches resulted in a number of 'hits', these being Operations Record Books for the Empire Central Flying School, 33 Maintenance Unit, Aston Down and the Ferry Training Unit. At the time I was a little unsure what information these may hold and in the case of 33 MU I was looking for mention of one particular Spitfire among hundreds held by the unit during that period of time. A long way to Kew from Coningsby, but the only way to find out what these records contained was to go and have a look.

At Kew I felt a certain weight of responsibility and awe handling these historic documents. The Operations Record Books themselves turned out to be a truly fascinating daily, weekly or monthly account of aspects of life on these units or stations, with matter of fact references to personnel, aircraft and equipment. Even tragic events, such as the loss of a pilot in a flying accident, were noted in a single line of simple text.

My first chosen document was that of the Empire Central Flying School and after leafing through a few pages there was TE311, under a heading of 'Allotment of Aircraft', along with a Seafire Mark 45 (LA465) on 3 October 1945 for handling trials. Although not mentioned by tail number, further entries referring to handling trials being carried out by a Spitfire XVI followed, under a number of headings of 'Special work carried out by the Squadron'. Also of significant interest was a paragraph stating that work had commenced on amendments to pilots' notes for the Spitfire IX, XI and XVI, to include the handling characteristics of these aircraft fitted with the rear tank. The final entry that appears to refer to TE311, states that a Spitfire XVI was allocated away to 39 MU on 18 February 1946. So here's the first anomaly, in that the movement card suggests TE311 went to 33 MU not 39 MU the day before. Unfortunately, I could not find a record for 39 MU or reference to the aircraft at 33 MU during that time. There was, however, mention of a Spitfire LF 16 in 33 MU's November 1953 entry. Then, in the December entry, there was TE311, the delayed Spitfire from the month before now complete. This, thankfully, is supported by the movement history, as TE311 apparently arrived at 33 MU in September of that year and left in January 1954, being transferred briefly to 2 CAACU (Civilian Anti-Aircraft Co-operation Unit) before returning late in February, eventually to be grounded and transferred to gate guardian duties at Tangmere in 1955.

So what of TE311's exploits with ferry training? Well there were two further mentions although the first was slightly misleading. The June 1951 entry for RAF Aston Down lists 'Spitfire Mk. 16 TF311' as being involved in an accident on 21 June 1951, the same date as TE311 was recorded as having her accident. Therefore, after subsequently finding no record of any Spitfires with a serial number starting with TF, I was confident that this was a simple typing error. The final mention I could find of TE311 came in April 1953 with her arrival at RAF Benson, along with another Spitfire (TB713), two Mosquitoes, two Harvards, two Lincolns and a Meteor following the disbandment of 1689 FPTF and the transfer of its work to the newly formed Ferry Training Unit located at Benson.

Towards the latter part of 2006 I was preparing to leave the service, so sadly did not progress the research further. However, I felt that Paul (and the BBMF) now had a reasonably accurate and cross-referenced potted history

of the aircraft from her construction to arrival at the Flight in 1999.

My advice for anyone undertaking research, is to make a source-referenced copy of everything you can that's relevant, have a little patience and cross reference any supposed facts as much as is possible and be prepared to accept that what you believed to be true, could at a later stage prove false; in other words don't force the jigsaw to fit your perception of fact from fiction; instead let the pieces fall naturally into place, even if that takes longer than planned.

Keeping originality or new-build?

In an ideal world you would like to keep your Spitfire as original as possible. However, with complete aircraft becoming harder to source, it means that the majority of the restoration, the wings and fuselage, will have to be built from new. This is achievable using authentic drawings and components as patterns. It could then be said that you are still retaining originality, but using a modern equivalent of war-time materials. For example, the skin of the aircraft was first made from Duralumin; the new equivalent skin is now created from an updated

RIGHT A fully equipped workshop is required for your Spitfire project. *(VMI Engineering)*

version of the same material. This also applies to the nuts, bolts and washers of the aircraft or AGS (aircraft general spares). Over the years the specs of these items have changed; for instance, bolts have altered their 'designation' from A15 to A25, although basically they are still the same item. It is these small differences that the potential restorer needs to be aware of when sourcing spares. If you can prove that the modern specifications have a link to the old ones then you can use that item. If you start changing material specs then it is deemed a modification.

Hazardous items, such as asbestos fireproof material (as used on frame 5, sandwiched between two skins) will have to be replaced with modern alternatives in order to comply with current health and safety regulations.

In the event of there being no original drawing for it, a component would need to be removed, cleaned and sent to the appropriate company, where it would then be examined, all relevant measurements taken, and then a technical drawing produced showing the part from every angle. This drawing would then be used to manufacture the component. This procedure is quite a common occurrence as there are only approximately 20,000 surviving drawings, covering all marks of Spitfire/Seafire.

While 20,000 drawings may seem a lot, given that there are 24 marks of Spitfire alone, plus the Seafire marks, and considering the many individual components within an aircraft, the restorer may find that the majority of these drawings may not be applicable to his aircraft at all. For example, out of these drawings there are only approximately 900 relating to the Spitfire Marks IX and XVI, although the aircraft does use certain drawings relevant to the marks prior to the Marks IX and XVI. This is an area

ABOVE AGS (Aircraft General Spares); nuts, bolts, washers, anchor nuts and split pins are just as important to source as some of the aircraft's components. *(Paul Blackah)*

LEFT This workshop belongs to VMI Engineering in Aldershot and has wing, fuselage, fin and tailplane jigs. *(VMI Engineering)*

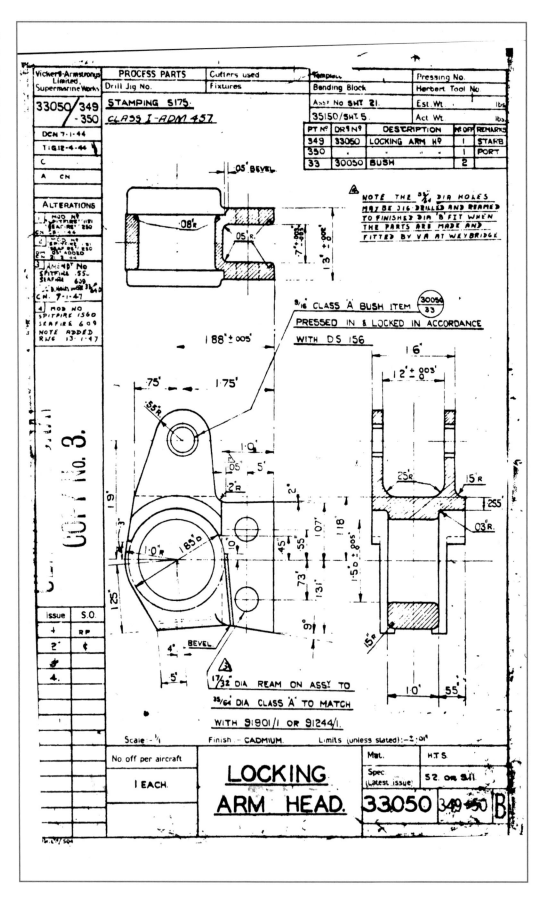

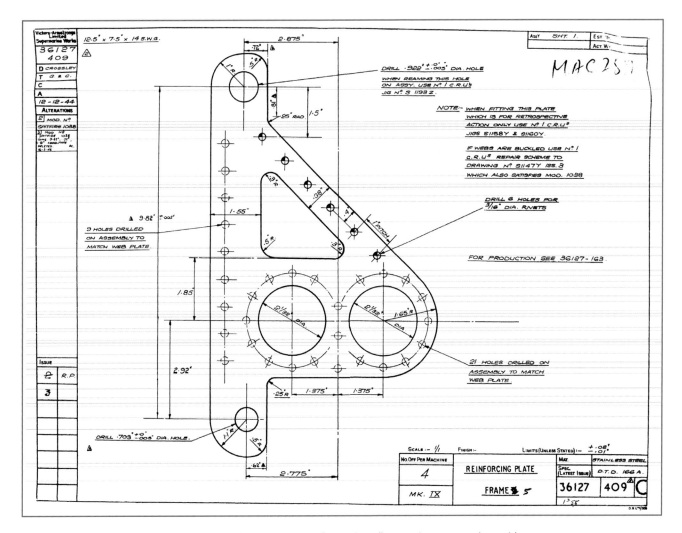

DRILL ·922"⁺·⁰"₋·⁰⁰⁵" DIA. HOLE

WHEN REAMING THIS HOLE
ON ASSY. USE N° 1 C.R.U⁵
JIG N° S 1198 Z.

NOTE:- WHEN FITTING THIS PLATE
WHICH IS FOR RETROSPECTIVE
ACTION ONLY USE N° 1 C.R.U⁵
JIGS S 1158Y & 91160Y.

IF WEBS ARE BUCKLED USE N° 1
C.R.U⁵ REPAIR SCHEME TO
DRAWING N° S 11 47Y ISS. 3
WHICH ALSO SATISFIES MOD. 1038

DRILL 6 HOLES FOR
³/₁₆" DIA. RIVETS

FOR PRODUCTION SEE 36127-163.

21 HOLES DRILLED ON
ASSEMBLY TO MATCH
WEB PLATE

9 HOLES DRILLED
ON ASSEMBLY TO
MATCH WEB PLATE.

DRILL ·703"⁺·⁰"₋·⁰⁰⁵" DIA. HOLE.

12·5" × 7·5" × 14 S.W.G.

Vickers-Armstrongs Limited
Supermarine Works
36127 409
D CROSSLEY
T G & C.
C
A
12-12-44
ALTERATIONS
2 MOD. N°
SATISFIES 1038

Issue

SCALE :- 1/1	Finish :-		LIMITS (UNLESS STATED) :- ⁺·⁰⁸"₋·⁰¹"
No. OFF PER MACHINE	REINFORCING PLATE	MAT.	STAINLESS STEEL
4		SPEC. (LATEST ISSUE)	D.T.D. 166 A.
MK. IX	FRAME 5	36127	409

where the restorer has to be careful to work to the correct information as you could easily end up paying for the manufacture of parts that were never fitted to your particular aircraft.

One instance where it is impossible to retain originality is with the aircraft's radio/avionics. With modern legislation, an aircraft has to be fitted with modern radios, IFF (Identification Friend or Foe) and Mode S, which allows it to be identified, when in the air, by Air Traffic Control.

Peter Monk is an owner/operator, who has now established his own company, based at Biggin Hill airfield. He gave us an insight into his operation and passion for the aircraft.

Peter has always been interested in the Spitfire and sees it as an iconic British design – every boy's dream to own and fly. In 1996 he was in the enviable position to buy his first restoration project, a Mark IX Spitfire (TA805),

which Peter describes as 'a scrapyard wreck'. It was an incomplete aircraft in very poor condition, but the potential was there. It took nine years before the plane was airworthy.

Once this aircraft was flying, and being serviced by outside companies, he realised that, as he was acquiring other Spitfires, he could set up his own company to restore, service and maintain not only his own, but others.

The Spitfire Company has been running successfully for some time and is an ideal set-up for the enthusiastic owner, an excellent example of how a childhood interest develops into something more tangible.

Peter now owns several Spitfires and a Hurricane. Two of the Spitfires, TA805 and a rare Mark I, X4650, are regularly seen on the air show circuit being flown by either Peter or one of his other pilots. Describing his experiences in the air he says he 'Feels at one with the aircraft, which is very easy to fly. There is a sense of

ABOVE Drawings are important to the project and many are held at the RAF Museum in Hendon. This one, 36127/409, is for a Mark IX or XVI.

ABOVE HF Mark IX, TA805, Peter Monk's scrapyard wreck restoration that took nine years to complete. (Clive Denney)

ABOVE HF Mark IX, TA805, Peter Monk's scrapyard wreck restoration that took nine years to complete. (Clive Denney)

BELOW The restored fuselage of Spitfire EP122. (Paul Blackah)

history every time I step into the cockpit and it is both a privilege and a joy to fly the Spitfire.'

He likes the aircraft to be as authentic as possible and, with that in mind, one of the biggest problems he has is the sourcing of original spares. His eye for detail is apparent when you take a look at his aircraft. For example, the Mark I's seat has the original armour plating in place, and even the engine starting handle is fitted and stowed on the back of the seat despite not being required.

His other aircraft are at various stages of completion and, with the right budget, they should take approximately three years to

complete, bearing in mind that other restorations are currently ongoing for clients, such as Mark XVI, RW382, Mark IX LZ 842 and Mark IX TD314. His restorations, some waiting to be started, include Mark V EP122, Mark IX TE517, Mark IX BR601 and Mark XVI TB885. At heart Peter will always be that young lad, running around the garden with his Spitfire held proudly aloft.

BELOW The CAA-approved serviceable label for Spitfire EP122, which was undergoing restoration at Biggin Hill by The Spitfire Company at the time of writing (2013). (Paul Blackah)

LEFT Spitfire Mark XVI, RW382, having a last clean prior to final inspection by the CAA. *(Paul Blackah)*

BELOW Spitfire Mark IX, TD314, nearing completion. *(Paul Blackah)*

Chapter Three

Stripping down and detailing components

Stripping down and detailing the aircraft's components is one of the most important phases of any restoration project; during this process you will establish what is reusable, what requires manufacturing – and what is missing! Just because you have a project, in whatever form it arrived in, it will not necessarily be complete. Also, you will discover if some of the component parts belong to, and are usable with, your particular mark of Spitfire. Once the components are sorted, the restorer will have a clearer idea of the next step forward.

OPPOSITE Fuselage paint stripped ready to be inspected for condition and damage. *(Paul Blackah)*

Initial assessment, possible costs etc

BELOW The cockpit prior to strip. *(Paul Blackah)*

BOTTOM The fuselage armour plate. Most restorers will not fit this as it adds unnecessary weight to the aircraft. *(Paul Blackah)*

Once a potential project has been sourced it is essential that the prospective purchaser arranges for an initial, independent assessment by a person or persons knowledgeable about the specific aircraft, in this case the Spitfire.

Included in this assessment should be a general overview of the condition of the aircraft, whether it is a complete one with all systems and components intact, just a large section of an aircraft, or if it is only a collection of frames, skins and components.

This assessment will include what is necessary to bring the aircraft back to flying or static condition depending on the owner's requirements. It may include recommendations as to specific companies specialising in airframe and engine work, and a rough estimate of cost and the problems faced if choosing a mark that has not been restored before.

In his role as Chief Technician of the RAF Battle of Britain Memorial Flight, and an expert authority on certain historic aircraft, including the Spitfire, co-author Paul Blackah was recently asked to provide a survey on a Spitfire Mark XXI, LA255. The report is a brief survey of the aircraft, condition and possible cost and is reproduced below as an indication of the type of report a potential owner could expect.

SURVEY OF MARK XXI SPITFIRE LA255, FEBRUARY 2012 BY CHIEF TECHNICIAN BLACKAH, MBE, RAF

Before I go into the details about the aircraft, the Mark XXI Spitfire was a major redesign of the normal Spitfire; the wings are significantly stiffened with smaller wingtips, the ailerons are about 8 inches longer and have a built-in trim tab, also the flaps are larger compared with earlier marks of Spitfire. Also, to improve handling, the undercarriage legs are placed further apart (7¾ inches) and the oleos were lengthened by 4½ inches, which enabled a larger diameter five-bladed prop to be fitted, 7 inches greater than the Mark XIX.

The aircraft was painted in gloss paint in the colours of 1 Squadron, although it is a completely inaccurate paint scheme. The paint was removed, leaving the aircraft in bare metal to further facilitate a thorough inspection.

The fuselage

The fuselage is in reasonable condition; however, the carry-through spars on frame 5 are damaged and there is corrosion on the frame 5 firewall, corrosion on the cockpit floor skin and fuel tank bay skins.

The windscreen is missing and has been replaced with a piece of thick Perspex, the canopy slider blocks are missing and a lot of

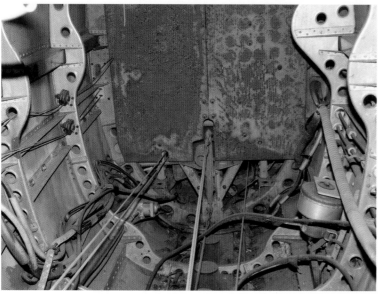

RIGHT Another view of the cockpit prior to strip.
(Paul Blackah)

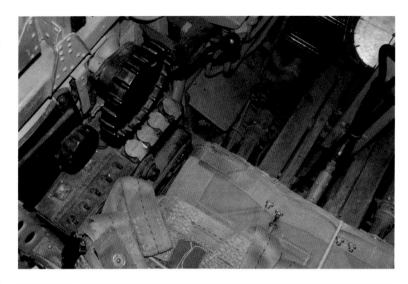

the fillet panel anchor nuts have drilled out rivets where screws should be fitted.

The fin unit has a tear in the skin around two of the access holes and it looks like the aircraft has been pulled backwards using these access panel holes. On the top of the fin, the skin is missing and has been replaced by blocks of shaped wood. The metal elevator and rudder are in not too bad condition.

The engine compartment

The engine bearers are complete, but the tubing is corroded. The Griffon engine is original, but all the pipe work for the oil and coolant systems is missing as is the coolant header tank, and the oil and fuel tanks. The propeller blades have been stripped of their protective finish as it was cracked and de-laminated. The prop hub is severely corroded and the spinner is badly dented.

The wings

I was unable to examine the internals of the wings as much as I would have liked, due to the fact that the original fasteners on the access panels had been removed and replaced by something that we could not identify or remove! I would suggest that they are modern fasteners off a Harrier or similar.

BELOW The undercarriage pintle and surrounding structure, again corroded. *(Paul Blackah)*

ABOVE With panels removed, the internal construction can be inspected. Here the gun bay is visible and many of the panel's receptacles are missing. *(Paul Blackah)*

LEFT The wing spar ends with attachment bolts. All the bolts require replacement as they are all damaged from years of being removed and refitted. *(Paul Blackah)*

The wings are quite badly corroded internally and the main spars are damaged where the wings have been removed and refitted over the years. The trailing edges are distorted and have a wavy appearance. Some of the inboard top skins are damaged.

Undercarriage

The oleos are corroded as are the undercarriage pintles and locking mechanisms, although they look sound. Both undercarriage jacks are damaged at the point where they connect to the undercarriage and the bodies are also corroded. The pipe work is complete, but covered in paint

so difficult to assess. The undercarriage door jacks are also corroded. The undercarriage doors are badly damaged as is the outer undercarriage door operating mechanism although the doors look sound. The tail leg is collapsed and corroded and it appears that the tail retraction jack is missing. All the wheels are corroded beyond use and the tyres perished.

Electrical system

All electrical wiring is no longer usable and all instruments have been removed due to being radioactive.

The way forward.

In order to restore to a presentable static condition the aircraft requires the corrosion on the wings and fuselage to be stabilised, to prevent further deterioration, by coating the inside of the fuselage and wings with a preventative. Minor repairs to be carried out on the damaged areas, for example the tail unit area, and, where possible, fit unserviceable, but non-radioactive instruments. Fit new, correct fasteners on access panels to give the appearance of correct assembly. Gag the undercarriage legs to prevent collapse and fit refurbished wheels and tyres. The aircraft would then require a complete respray.

This work would cost upwards of £5,000, which does not take into account man hours.

To restore to flight, the aircraft would require an extensive strip and rebuild, replacing all items such as wiring, pipe work for oil, coolant and hydraulic systems. New propeller blades and hub, new engine or the old one overhauled. Wing spars replacing, frame 5 replacing, all magnesium rivets, along with any skins and frames that are found damaged during the strip. All hydraulic and pneumatic components will require overhaul or replacing.

This work would cost upwards of £750,000.

As can be seen, the above report is only a very basic one and doesn't reflect what may be found if the aircraft were dismantled. The decision to purchase would be made on the basis of a similar written or even a simple verbal report.

Where to do it, who to do it – could you do it yourself?

The first decision that you need to make is who is going to carry out the restoration work. Are you able to do this yourself, do you require an outside agency, or do you want to be involved at some level in the project?

A huge consideration must be the fact that, if the aircraft is being restored to flying specifications, then whoever is working on the aircraft either has to be licensed by the CAA or, at the very least, have a licensed engineer to sign off the work that has been carried out.

It is possible, with no engineering experience and no general understanding of the workings of an aircraft, to still become hands-on involved in a restoration project. This would be done under the supervision of your licensed engineer, who could guide you through the processes; for example, stripping and cleaning individual items or reassembling. This gives a great feeling of achievement and involvement in your project and it becomes much more personal to you.

The choice is down to the owner of the project whether to be involved, or to hand the project over to a specialist company or an individual experienced in dealing with restoration projects, who would then take charge and deliver a completed aircraft, hopefully within the time frame agreed.

Managing the project yourself is not as simple as you may first think. There are considerations that need addressing even before your aircraft arrives. If you were restoring it yourself, you would need a large enough building to work in and have to decide whether

BELOW Elevator framework. *(VMI Engineering)*

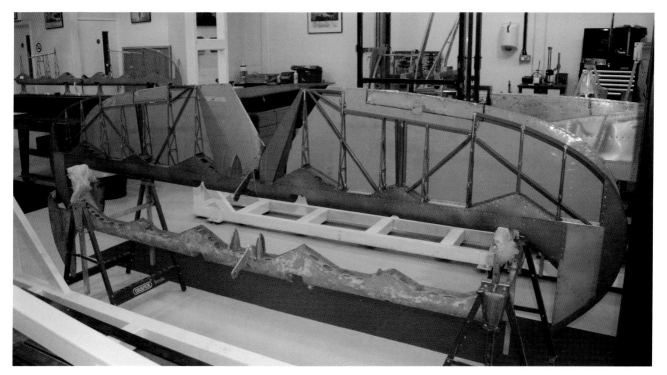

it would eventually be assembled at these premises or sent elsewhere for this stage of the restoration. And if your building was not on an airfield you would have to transport your aircraft to another location in order to operate it.

The main consideration, prior to stripping your aircraft, is to have in place the specialised equipment necessary in order to facilitate the strip and rebuild. These items, such as a fuselage and pair of wing jigs and engine stand, would have to be purchased, built or manufactured according to your aircraft's requirements. These items will be expensive and you must factor in these costs and decide whether they are ones you want to incur if you are only going to use them once. For example, each wing jig could cost up to £15,000 and a fuselage jig up to £30,000.

If considering manufacturing components, such as skins, frames and spars, then you would not only need the relevant equipment, but also require the appropriate accreditations from the CAA. Restoring a classic aircraft may appear as simple as renovating a classic car, with regards to the stripping, cleaning, having parts manufactured and subsequently

reassembling; however, a classic car simply requires a trained mechanic to look it over and sign the MoT and the job is done. An aircraft, with all the risks to public safety that flight entails, requires paperwork for every item manufactured as well as the relevant licensing and accreditations for those working on the aircraft, and visits by the CAA to check for quality standards, correct procedure and paperwork. Giving your project over to a specialist allows you to bypass all the aggravation while retaining the control!

To summarise: you could do the project yourself, but at a lot of extra cost. Yet you could still be hands-on with your project by helping to strip and rebuild, having had the major components restored by accredited companies. The other option is to hand over your project entirely and wait until the finished aircraft is returned to you.

Stripping down

The sensible way to begin your project is to draw up a plan of action based on your initial assessment. Included in said plan would

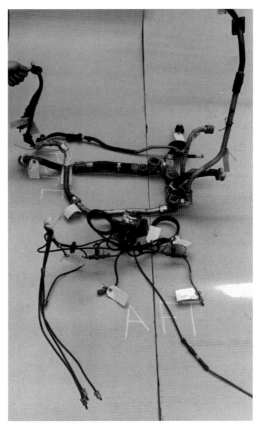

FAR LEFT The cockpit prior to strip. Years of dirt and debris will need to be cleared out after the strip so that the inspection can be carried out. *(RAF BBMF)*

LEFT Laying out a system after removal, labelling and taking photos is essential. *(RAF BBMF)*

be the outside agencies that you would need to use, the approximate timescale (which inevitably changes as snags arise), equipment needed and where to source it, manpower and also how to go about acquiring your stage checks and who would be licensed to do this for you. So, assuming you have all this in hand and a relatively complete aircraft to start with, it's time to begin!

Before removing any components or systems, it is good practice to take as many photographs as possible. This will allow the restorer to see how the respective parts are fitted and, for example, how the cabling and pipework are routed and where they are clipped into position. It will also show how other components are positioned in relation to each other; for instance, how the instruments are fitted to the instrument panel, which instruments are fitted from behind the panel, which have spacers to make them stand out etc. Although this information can be sourced through using original drawings, a photograph will complement the information on a technical drawing and give the restorer another point of information.

LEFT Fuselage stripped and ready for inspection. *(RAF BBMF)*

How do I know which mark of Spitfire I have?

The aircraft has data plates in various places, such as in the cockpit of the fuselage, under the datum longeron, or on the frame 5 engine bulkhead. These two plates have information stamped on them that tell you where the aircraft was built, eg CBAF, which means Castle Bromwich Aircraft Factory, and a serial number indicating the production number of the aircraft. So CBAF 23 would mean the aircraft was the 23rd one produced at Castle Bromwich. Under this figure is the aircraft type drawing number, eg 30027, which shows the plate is from a Mark I (indicated by the '300') and that the part is from the fuselage (denoted by the '27').

The following table is of great use to the restorer, but it is not a definitive table although it does reflect the most popular marks of Spitfire.

BREAKDOWN OF SPITFIRE DRAWING NUMBERS	
Drawing number	Aircraft mark
300	Mark I
325	Mark II
330	Mark III
337	Mark IV
331	Mark Vb
349	Mark Vc
350	Mark VI
351	Mark VII
359	Mark VIII
361	Marks IX/XVI
362	Mark X
365	Mark PRXI
366	Mark XII
367	Mark PRXIII
369/372/373/379	Mark XIV
394	Mark XVIII
389/390	Mark XIX
356	Marks 21, 22 and 24
357	Seafire Mark II
358	Seafire Mark III
377	Seafire Mark XV
384	Seafire Mark XVII
388	Seafire Marks 45 to 47
502	Mark VIII trainer
509	Mark IX trainer
518	Mark XVIII trainer

RIGHT The data and mod plates will give information on which mark you have and what modifications have been carried out on this item, in this case the fuselage. *(Paul Blackah)*

RIGHT A wing mod plate and data plate from a Mark IX. It records all the modifications that have been embodied into the wing stamped upon it. *(Paul Blackah)*

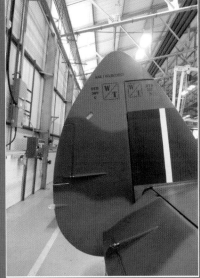

Rudders come in different sizes depending on the mark of Spitfire. Here are three of the most common: small for the Mark II, medium for the Mark XVI and large on a Mark XIX. *(Paul Blackah)*

Stripping out the aircraft

For the benefit of this book, we will assume that your aircraft has been delivered with the wings already removed, as this will generally be the case with all non-flying restoration projects.

To aid with the process of stripping down, you should make sure you have the relevant air publications for your mark of Spitfire. The Vol I *Servicing and Descriptive Handbook* will be very useful in this process. There are chapters with diagrams on the removing of flying controls, the engine, the wings, fuel systems etc. This book is not the only publication you will require during the strip down and rebuild. Each mark of Spitfire has its own suite of books, which are broken down as follows, with the Spitfire Mark IX/XVI aircraft being used by way of an example.

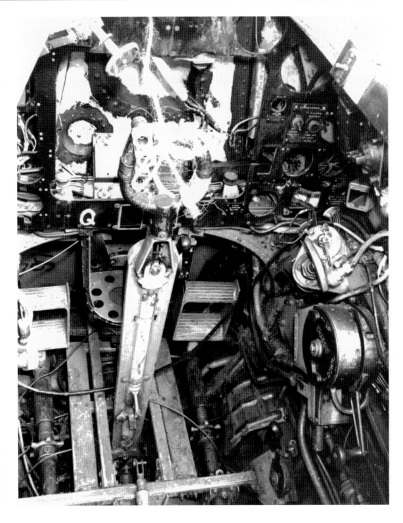

RIGHT Before removing systems from the cockpit the restorer should take as many pictures as possible to aid with the rebuild. This cockpit belongs to a Mark XIX (PS915). *(RAF BBMF)*

Vol 1   *Servicing and Descriptive Handbook*:
         AP1565J and L.

Vol 2   *Part 1 – Modification leaflets.*
         This part is broken down into 17
         subsections as follows:
         A Aerofoils (control surfaces)
         B Undercarriage
         C Armament
         D Controls
         E Cooling system
         F Electrical equipment
         G Engine starting
         H Fuel system
         J Fuselage
         K Instruments
         L Jigs and tools
         M Miscellaneous equipment
         N Oil system
         O Oxygen system
         P Power plant
         Q Wireless equipment
         Z Modification leaflet
         Note – not all of these sections will be
         relevant to your rebuild.

Vol 2   *Part 2.*
         Consists of three sections as follows:
         Section 1   Between-flight inspections
         Section 2   Daily inspections
         Section 3   Minor and major inspections
         Note – these sections will be useful
         when it comes to organising your

servicing schedule for approval by
the CAA.

Vol 2   *Part 3 – User unit repairs.*
         These are repairs that would have
         been carried out at a squadron/station
         level and consists of the following nine
         'chapters'.
         Chapter 1   General information
         Chapter 2   Engine mounting
         Chapter 3   Systems
         Chapter 4   Fuselage
         Chapter 5   Alighting gear
         Chapter 6   Mainplanes
         Chapter 7   Tailplane
         Chapter 8   Elevator and rudder
         Chapter 9   Miscellaneous

Vol 2   *Part 4.*
         This section contains the major repair
         schemes and is broken down into nine
         groups.
         Group A   General information
         Group B   Engine mounting
         Group C   Systems
         Group D   Fuselage
         Group E   Alighting gear
         Group F   Mainplanes
         Group G   Tailplane
         Group H   Elevator and rudder
         Group J   Miscellaneous

Vol 3   *Part 1* is the schedule of spare parts

Vol 3   *Part 2* is the appendix A

BELOW AP1565, Vol
II, detailing the metal
thickness on the
mainplane skins.

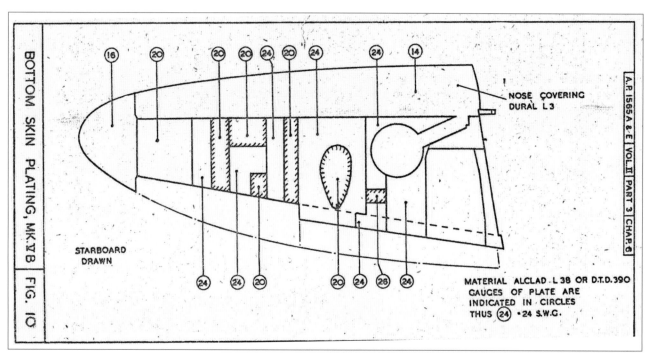

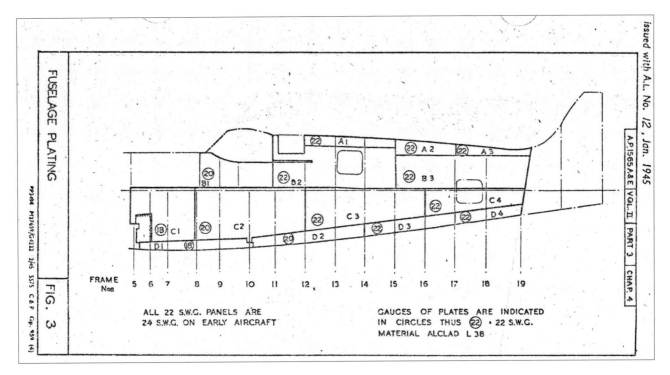

FUSELAGE PLATING

FIG. 3

FRAME Nos

ALL 22 S.W.G. PANELS ARE
24 S.W.G. ON EARLY AIRCRAFT

GAUGES OF PLATES ARE INDICATED
IN CIRCLES THUS ㉒ · 22 S.W.G.
MATERIAL ALCLAD L 38

Further to the main three volumes are a host of other AP designations that cover the rest of the equipment. The main range of books are as follows, although there are others if you wish to do such things as fitting working machine guns and carrying bombs etc:

AP2240A	Aero-engines
AP2241	Fuel pumps in aero-engines
AP1590P, S and U	Merlin 66/70 manual
AP2616D	Packard Merlin 266
AP1095 series	Electrical equipment
AP1803N	Hydraulic equipment
AP1275A and B	Instruments, general and navigational
AP2337	Wheels, tyres and brakes

It should be noted that the AP1565 series of manuals only cover the Spitfire Mark I (1565A) to the Mark XIX (1565W) and you may need several different marks of Spitfire manuals to cover the version you are restoring as, in certain marks, reference is made to earlier models of Spitfire. For example, in the AP1565W for the Mark XIX, the chapter relating to the fuselage refers you to the AP1565T, which is for the Mark XIV.

From Spitfire Mark 21 to Mark 24 the publications are the AP2816 series, A to C, and if you are restoring a Seafire the series of manuals you require are the AP2280 series, A to G – the A being the Seafire Mark I and the G being the Seafire Mark 46/47.

Where engines are concerned, the Merlin requires the AP1590 series of books, plus, if you are using a Packard engine, the AP2616 series of manuals. For the Griffon engines it is the AP2234 series of manuals. Again, as with the Spitfire marks, each engine model has its own unique identification code. For example, a Merlin 66 uses the AP1590P, S and U manuals and a Griffon 61 uses the AP2234K manuals.

Stripping the aircraft needs to be done in a methodical, planned manner, with each system being dismantled separately. Firstly, all cowlings, access panels and fillet fairings should be removed and all screws and fasteners bagged and kept with the associated panels. Next would be the propeller, engine and engine bearer (assuming that these are included). This would enable the oil and coolant pipework system to be taken apart – again all clamps, fittings and fasteners should be kept with the associated parts – and also give you access to the hydraulic components that are fitted on frame 5.

The next step is to remove the top and bottom fuel tanks and the related pipework. Hopefully the restorer is remembering to take photographs throughout each step; these will be invaluable when it comes to refitting.

ABOVE AP1565, Vol II, which details the fuselage skin plates and their gauge thickness.

RIGHT The lower engine cowling has had filler applied to hide dents and holes. This was only found when the paint was removed. *(Paul Blackah)*

BELOW The Griffon engine bearer, which is different in construction to the tubed Merlin one. *(Paul Blackah)*

ABOVE The bottom fuel tank still has its original rubberised covering on, but when removed the tank was corroded beyond repair. *(Paul Blackah)*

BELOW Inside the fuselage prior to strip. The flying control cables and air bottles will need replacing due to age and condition. *(Paul Blackah)*

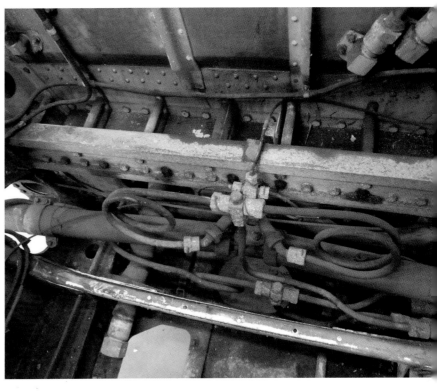

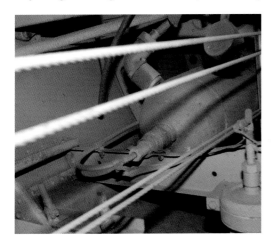

ABOVE The fuel tank bay of the fuselage, again quite heavily corroded. The retraction jacks and pipework are also badly corroded. *(Paul Blackah)*

LEFT The fin unit removed from the fuselage awaiting inspection. *(Paul Blackah)*

The following systems should then be disassembled: the hydraulic, pneumatic, elevator, rudder, elevator trim and rudder trim control runs, instrument panel and gauges, the wiring harness and all associated electrical equipment. The oxygen system should be removed, if fitted, followed by the fin assembly complete with tailplanes (this would include the rudder and elevator).

By completing these steps, the fuselage should be completely stripped out and ready to go into a fuselage jig in order for the fuselage itself to be stripped down to examine individual skins, frames and longerons.

LEFT Coolant and oil pipes. These will be cleaned, pressure tested and utilised again or will be used as patterns to produce new pipes. *(Paul Blackah)*

RIGHT This wing is being inspected and it is surprising what you can find: here is a bird's nest being removed! *(RAF BBMF)*

Wings

After the fuselage is stripped the next task is to remove the systems out of the wings. These include the radiators, oil cooler, pneumatic piping, gun heating piping, aileron control system and undercarriage system. The flaps, aileron and wingtip should also be dismantled, along with all access panels. The wing is now ready for inspection and assessment. Components and their respective fasteners should be bagged and kept together, and more photographs please.

The process of stripping down components varies according to what you are working with and some examples follow.

The rudder and elevator

In order for the ribs and framework of the rudder and elevator to be examined, the fabric covering must be taken off. As the fabric is held in place by stitching around the ribs, the easiest way to remove the fabric is to cut into it and draw it back carefully until you

RIGHT With the flap open it shows some ribs missing and the wing skin and ribs have damage as well as corrosion. *(Paul Blackah)*

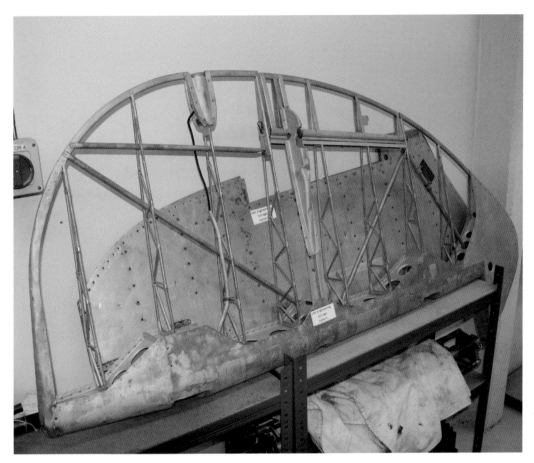

LEFT Rudder framework, behind which can be seen the metal skin for an elevator. Metal skinned elevators were fitted to Spitfires equipped with rear fuselage fuel tanks. *(VMI Engineering)*

BELOW Rebuilt elevator requiring new fabric covering. *(Paul Blackah)*

RIGHT Leading
edge skins removed
from the wings. (Paul
Blackah)

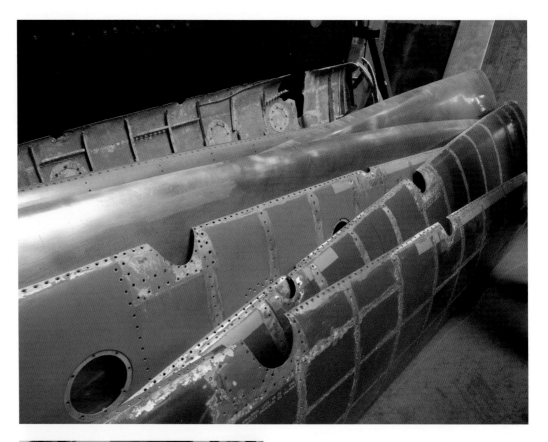

reach one of the ribs. Then snip the stitching and peel back again until you reach another rib, repeating the process until the task is complete. If you don't cut the stitching around the ribs and simply attempt to pull the fabric straight off, the ribs could easily distort or crack. However, on the leading edge and the horn of the rudder the fabric can just be pulled off as it is only stuck in place. Once the fabric is removed the rudder and elevator are now ready for inspection.

Assessing the major structure of the aircraft

The fuselage, once stripped out, is relatively easy to assess, as you can see all the frames, intercostals, longerons and skins. What you can't see is what is going on between the skin and the frames and also the few areas that have limited access. To inspect these areas thoroughly the skin would require removing.

So what are you actually looking for? Primarily, the obvious corrosion and cracking of skins and frames and any distortion to

the fuselage, which could, for example, have happened while the aircraft was in storage. You are also searching for any repairs that have been carried out to skins and frames. Another area of concern would be the carry-through spars on frame 5 – are the wing attachment holes elongated or out of limits (meaning, have the holes become too big to accept the original bolts)? In the opinion of the authors, these carry-through spars should be replaced as a matter of course when restoring a Spitfire – after all, they do hold the wings on!

Once this survey on the fuselage has been carried out, you should have a good understanding of its condition and whether you have any frames or skins that require replacing. It is now the individual's choice as to whether the entire fuselage is sent away to be refurbished by one of the expert companies in this field, or whether to tackle the work yourself.

The wings must undergo a similar inspection to the fuselage: assessing the skins and ribs, again for corrosion, distortion and cracking. The

ABOVE Inside the stripped fuselage from frame 19, looking forward. *(Paul Blackah)*

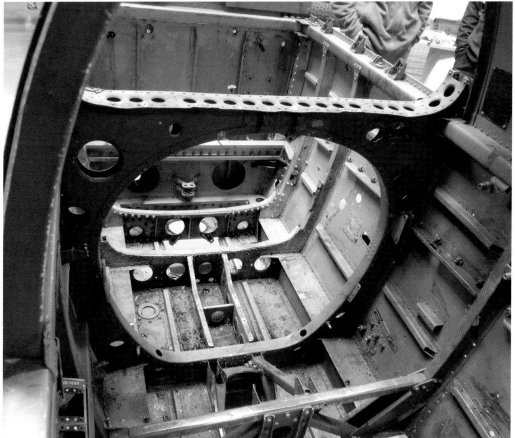

LEFT Cockpit stripped out enabling the skins and internal structures to be examined. *(Paul Blackah)*

wing spars, because of their construction, are difficult to inspect and, regardless of condition, like the carry-through spars on the fuselage they should be replaced as a matter of course. Once again, it is dependent on the individual's expertise as to whether they tackle the refurbishment themselves, or send the wings away to a specialist company.

The fin and the tailplanes should be examined in the same manner as the fuselage and wings.

Inspecting the system components

The larger components, such as undercarriage legs, retraction jacks, elevator, rudder and engine bearer, to name but a few, will need to be stripped down further for inspection. Each system has its own unique set of drawing numbers; for instance, in the drawing number 36145 the '361' shows that it is from a Mark IX or a Mark XVI and the '45' indicates that it is from the fuel system. The following table has a few examples of the numbering system for the components of the aircraft.

SYSTEMS, COMPONENTS AND THEIR DRAWING NUMBERS	
System/component	Drawing number
Main planes	30008
Tailplane	30018
Fuselage	30027
Elevator	30020
Ailerons	30012
Rudder	30023
Tail wheel	30026
Undercarriage/hydraulics	30050
Instruments	30034
Radiators	30041
Oil system	30047
Fuel tanks	30044
Oil tank	30046
Header tank	30048
Engine cowlings	30038
Electrical equipment	30036
Fuel system	30045
Flaps	30069
Engine controls	30039
Trim control	30066
Pneumatics	30059
Engine mounting	30037

BELOW The undercarriage leg showing the up and down-locks. The leg requires stripping and any corrosion will need removing. Once removed, it will need to be checked to see if it is still within prescribed limits. *(Paul Blackah)*

Undercarriage legs/oleos

These are stripped by first removing the axle assembly, which is held on by two or three bolts, depending on the mark of Spitfire. The air charging point, which is located at the top of the leg, is loosened to allow the leg to be depressurised. This is essential, as if not done when the gland nut is unscrewed the pressure will force out the remaining oil – which will potentially cover you, the floor and anyone nearby with hydraulic oil! The gland nut is then unfastened and removed and any oil drained off.

Again, depending on the mark of Spitfire undercarriage leg/oleo, the plunger tube, complete with seals, is withdrawn from the undercarriage body. On early marks this is done by unscrewing six bolts, which holds in a splined fitting; when the bolts are removed the plunger tube comes out, complete with the splined fitting. On later marks the plunger tube is just pulled straight out and there is no internal splined fitting.

Inspecting components for viability

ABOVE Wing framework ready for inspection. Depending on the condition these will either be replaced or refitted. *(VMI Engineering)*

BELOW Typical skin damage from years of neglect. *(Paul Blackah)*

Once the aircraft is stripped down to its component parts, the task of inspecting and assessing can begin in earnest. Let's take a brief look at the individual parts and run through some of the checks that are required.

Skins, frames and ribs

The skins, frames and ribs will be individually examined for cracks, corrosion, dents, holes and elongated rivet holes; this will be done by eye. Small cracks can be dressed out (removed by filing) if the item is not structurally significant. Small dents can also be dressed out (by using a specialised hammer). Corrosion can be removed, either chemically or by sanding, and if it is light surface corrosion it may be possible to save the panel or rib. However, should the corrosion be more substantial, then the panel, rib or frame should be replaced, because one would end up removing too much of the material.

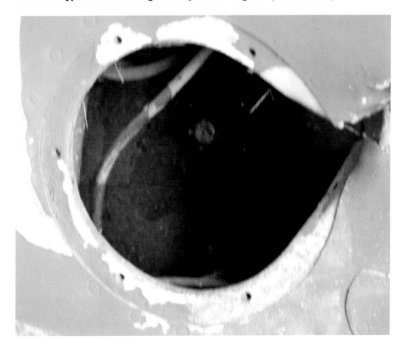

RIGHT Fuselage skins removed exposing the frames. *(Paul Blackah)*

BELOW Wing rib and wing components await inspection for cracks and elongated holes. *(VMI Engineering)*

If not too bad, elongated holes can be drilled out to the next rivet size up. There is a limit to how often this can be done before the item needs replacing or repairing. A good aid in any of these checks is to have available the relevant AP1565 (Vol 2, Parts 3 and 4 repair manual). This book details the acceptable limits of dents, cracks, holes and corrosion. These are broken down into three categories:

Negligible damage – On engine bearer tubes this means smooth dents that are free from cracking or any sharp edges, provided they are not deeper than the thickness of the tube in which they are found. Bowed tubes are allowed providing they are not greater than 0.03in. A bow and a dent in one tube, in certain tubes of the engine bearer, could be considered negligible damage.

On skins, negligible damage would be deemed as above, except where the line of riveting has been disturbed by the damage.

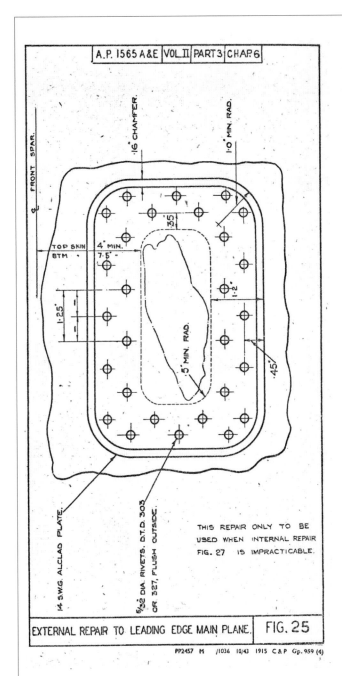

EXTERNAL REPAIR TO LEADING EDGE MAIN PLANE. FIG. 25

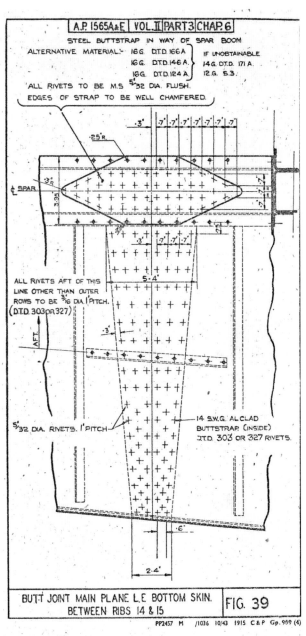

BUTT JOINT MAIN PLANE L.E BOTTOM SKIN. BETWEEN RIBS 14 & 15 FIG. 39

Damage repairable by patching – If the damage is greater than negligible damage, then it may be possible to carry out a patch repair, although if you are restoring the aircraft this option should only be used when you are operating the aircraft, where a quick repair is required. However, the choice is yours; if you want to use as much original material as possible you may feel that a patch repair is the way to go. These repairs are laid out in the repair manuals for the aircraft mark.

Damage requiring replacement – If the damage is greater than that practicable for patching, then the part will require replacing. In the case of an engine bearer it may be possible to replace a tube, but keep the end fittings original, providing the latter are still in good enough condition after removing the tube. Likewise, if you replace a skin because of excessive damage you may be able to keep the intercostals and framework if they are not affected and are in a serviceable condition after inspection.

ABOVE Repair schemes that can be used if damage is found.

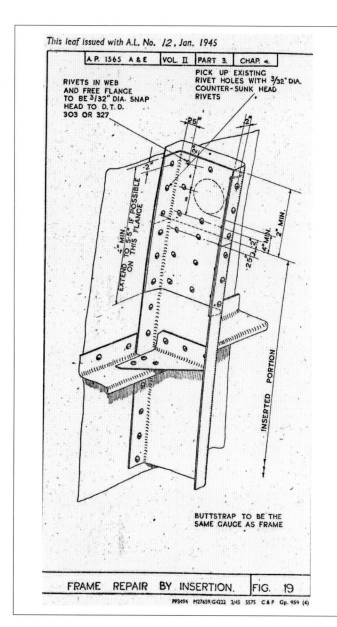

This leaf issued with A.L. No. 12, Jan. 1945

| A.P. 1565 A & E | VOL. II | PART. 3. | CHAP. 4. |

PICK UP EXISTING
RIVET HOLES WITH ³/₃₂" DIA.
COUNTER-SUNK HEAD
RIVETS

RIVETS IN WEB
AND FREE FLANGE
TO BE ³/₃₂" DIA. SNAP
HEAD TO D.T.D.
303 OR 327

EXTEND TO 5.5" IF POSSIBLE
ON THIS FLANGE

INSERTED PORTION

BUTTSTRAP TO BE THE
SAME GAUGE AS FRAME

| FRAME REPAIR BY INSERTION. | FIG. 19 |

PP3494 M27659/G4222 2/45 5575 C & P Gp. 959 (4)

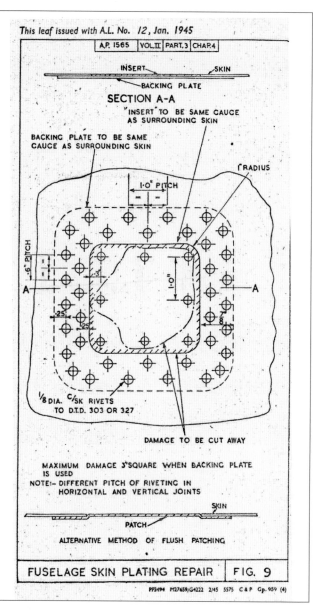

This leaf issued with A.L. No. 12, Jan. 1945

| A.P. 1565 | VOL.II | PART. 3 | CHAP.4 |

INSERT — SKIN
BACKING PLATE

SECTION A-A

"INSERT" TO BE SAME GAUGE
AS SURROUNDING SKIN

BACKING PLATE TO BE SAME
GAUGE AS SURROUNDING SKIN

RADIUS

1·0" PITCH

6" PITCH

1·0"

·25
·125

⅛" DIA. C/SK RIVETS
TO D.T.D. 303 OR 327

DAMAGE TO BE CUT AWAY

MAXIMUM DAMAGE 3"SQUARE WHEN BACKING PLATE
IS USED
NOTE:- DIFFERENT PITCH OF RIVETING IN
HORIZONTAL AND VERTICAL JOINTS

SKIN

PATCH

ALTERNATIVE METHOD OF FLUSH PATCHING

| FUSELAGE SKIN PLATING REPAIR | FIG. 9 |

PP3494 M27659/G4222 2/45 5575 C & P Gp. 959 (4)

ABOVE AND OPPOSITE Further repair schemes.

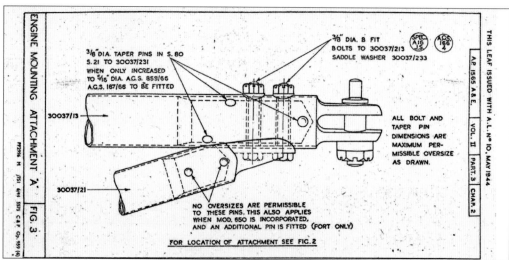

ENGINE MOUNTING ATTACHMENT 'A'.

³/₈" DIA. B FIT
BOLTS TO 30037/213
SADDLE WASHER 30037/233

³/₈" DIA. TAPER PINS IN S. 80
S. 21 TO 30037/231
WHEN ONLY INCREASED
TO ⁵/₁₆" DIA. A.G.S. 859/66
A.G.S. 167/66 TO BE FITTED

30037/13

30037/21

ALL BOLT AND
TAPER PIN
DIMENSIONS ARE
MAXIMUM PER-
MISSIBLE OVERSIZE
AS DRAWN.

NO OVERSIZES ARE PERMISSIBLE
TO THESE PINS. THIS ALSO APPLIES
WHEN MOD. 650 IS INCORPORATED,
AND AN ADDITIONAL PIN IS FITTED (PORT ONLY)

FOR LOCATION OF ATTACHMENT SEE FIG.2

| FIG. 3. |

THIS LEAF ISSUED WITH A.L. Nº 10, MAY 1944

A.P. 1565 A.& E. | VOL. II | PART.3 | CHAP. 2

RIGHT Detail of the engine bearer.

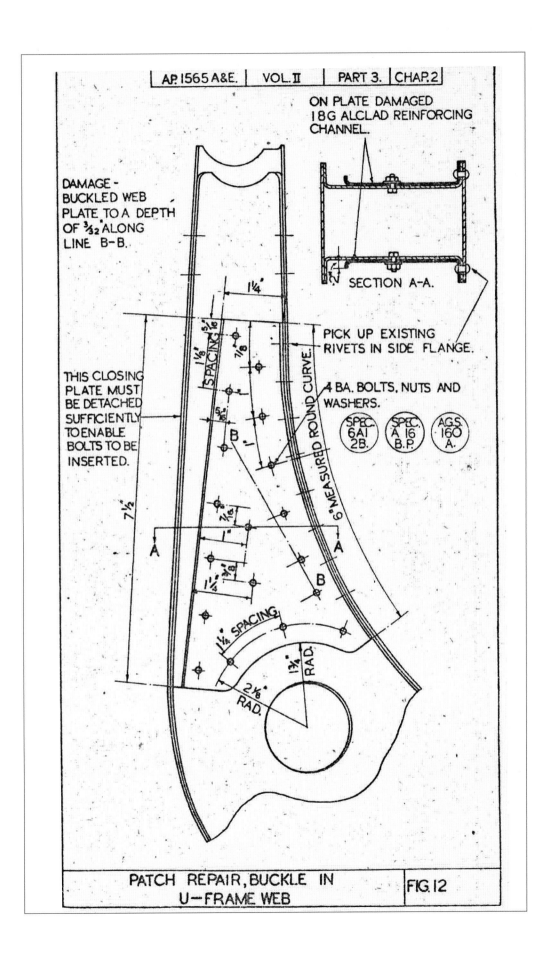

AP. 1565 A&E. | VOL. II | PART 3. | CHAP. 2

ON PLATE DAMAGED 18G ALCLAD REINFORCING CHANNEL.

SECTION A-A.

DAMAGE - BUCKLED WEB PLATE TO A DEPTH OF $\frac{3}{32}$" ALONG LINE B-B.

THIS CLOSING PLATE MUST BE DETACHED SUFFICIENTLY TO ENABLE BOLTS TO BE INSERTED.

PICK UP EXISTING RIVETS IN SIDE FLANGE.

4 BA. BOLTS, NUTS AND WASHERS.

SPEC. 6A1 2B. | SPEC. A16 B.P. | A.G.S. 160 A.

$1\frac{1}{4}$"

SPACING

$\frac{5}{16}$"

$\frac{7}{8}$"

$1\frac{1}{8}$"

$\frac{5}{16}$"

1"

B

6" MEASURED ROUND CURVE.

$7\frac{1}{2}$"

A

$\frac{7}{8}$"

1"

A

$1\frac{1}{4}$"

$\frac{7}{8}$"

B

$1\frac{1}{2}$" SPACING

$1\frac{3}{4}$" RAD.

$2\frac{1}{8}$" RAD.

PATCH REPAIR, BUCKLE IN U—FRAME WEB | FIG. 12

As mentioned, the repair manual is a guide. If you want to keep as much original material as possible in your project, care must be taken with the items that you choose to repair. This is simply because the aircraft could not only end up looking like a patchwork quilt, but also because there are weight limitations for every mark of Spitfire and repairs can affect the aircraft's centre of gravity and overall weight. This in turn impacts on the aircraft's performance and handling and could mean that it is not allowed to fly.

The manual states all the limits for repairs, metal specifications and rivet sizes. Deviate from these and you would have to submit a repair scheme to a stress engineer to ensure that it would be fit for purpose, and authorisation for use would have to be applied for by the Civil Aviation Authority.

Because of their construction, items such as main spars and the engine bearer will need NDT (non-destructive testing) carried out on them to check for corrosion and cracking. This is done by using an X-ray technique.

The engine bearer and main spar attachment have holes, which bolt them to the aircraft. These holes will also need inspecting; in the case of the

engine bearer to check that the taper is within limits, or the bolt will just fall through and new fittings will be required. With the wing spars the top spar has three bolt holes and the bottom one has four; these need to be checked for wear and ovality. These are particularly important as the allowance from the nominal size is just eight bolt sizes over this, in increments of four thousandths of an inch, a total of thirty-two thousandths of an inch. If the holes are over the upper tolerance, then the main spar needs replacing, or repairing by 'sleeving' the holes with the approval of the CAA.

Electrical wiring

Once the wiring harness has been removed from the fuselage and wings, if you have managed to get it out as a complete system you should remove any wiring that you know you will not be going to install – for example, the gun system – and then use the original wiring to help you make up a new wiring harness for the aircraft. If the aircraft doesn't have any wiring at all, or it has been cut away and taken out, then the wiring harness will be fitted to the aircraft during assembly and the correct routing and length will be sorted during this process.

Instruments

Instruments should be handled with care and should be checked to make sure that all the glass is intact, as these gauges are radioactive and there is a risk that broken glass could allow you to breathe in radioactive dust.

Hydraulic components

All the hydraulic components, undercarriage selector, retraction jacks, relief valves, filters and the hydraulic reservoir, should be stripped down and checked for general condition (dents and cracks), internal corrosion and condition. Consider replacing all rubber seals, as after long periods of inactivity the seals will probably have perished.

Retraction jack bodies should be pressure tested at one and a half times the aircraft's system pressure. The aircraft hydraulic pressure is 1,200psi, so items are tested at 1,800psi to ensure there are no leaks around any of the soldered joints. A manual, 1803N series, is essential as it lays down test procedures and fits and clearances of these components.

Undercarriage

Undercarriage legs and tail leg strut should be stripped and examined in the same way as the retraction jack, the main difference being that you are checking for corrosion on the fesculised (shiny) portion of the sustaining ram. If the corrosion or pitting is too deep then they will need replacing; if not they can be rechromed. They also should be inspected for straightness.

Axles should be non-destructive tested by using a mag particle check, to ensure that the wheel bearing surfaces are not cracked.

NDT – NON-DESTRUCTIVE TESTING

There are four methods of non-destructive testing that are available to the restorer. These are carried out by specialist companies or by trained individuals who are authorised to carry out these tests and are re-certified on a regular basis. Tests such as those including X-rays, are undertaken by a larger company with the appropriate equipment. The methods are as follows:

X-ray checks

X-rays are used to examine parts of the Spitfire that cannot be easily accessed, such as the main spars and the engine bearer tubing. This check will usually show up any internal corrosion or cracking on these components. Very careful examination of the results is necessary to interpret the X-ray film.

Ultrasound checks

This check uses sound waves to detect cracking around the bore of a hole and will be used on, for example, the main spar holes. A probe is inserted into the hole and a meter readout indicates if there are any signs of damage in the vicinity of the hole.

Magnetic particle check

This method is used to look for cracks in ferrous metal components, such as undercarriage pintle bearing surfaces and main undercarriage axle bearing surfaces. The component is painted with a fluid containing iron filings and then an electrical current is passed through it. The sample is then examined under ultra-violet light, which highlights any faults. Afterwards, the sample is demagnetised.

Die penetrant check

This is the one method that does not use any specialist equipment, which means that a trained individual can easily carry out the test. It is used for identifying cracks in ferrous and non-ferrous metal components. The kit consists of three tins. 1. The dye. This is purple, is painted on to the area to be tested and left. 2. The solvent. The dye is cleaned off using the solvent/cleaner. 3. The developer. The developer is sprayed on to the clean area, which coats it with a white film. This is left on for approximately 40 minutes and if there is a crack the developer will draw out the dye and this will be your indication, highlighted in purple.

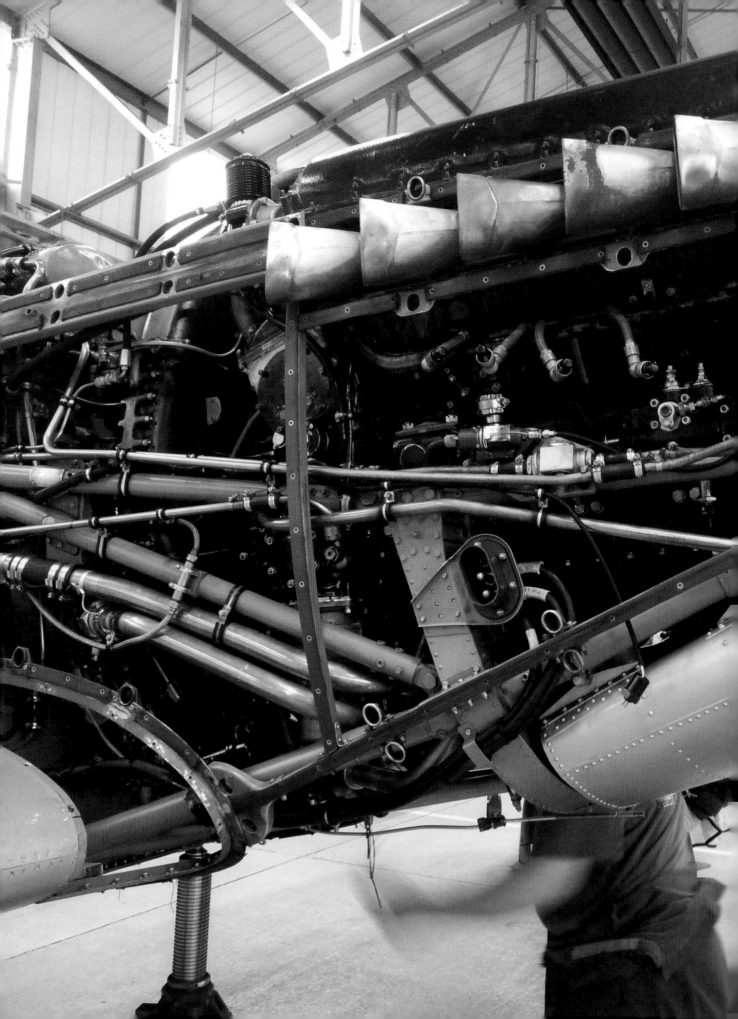

Chapter Four

Engine and propeller

Two of the most important parts of your project are the engine and propeller. Without these major components your aircraft will not be complete. In this chapter we take a look at the different types of engines and propellers, how to restore an original back to flying condition, and the companies that are able to offer these services.

OPPOSITE The engine installation on a **Spitfire Mark IX complete with the cowling rail framework to which the engine cowlings are attached.** *(Paul Blackah)*

ABOVE LEFT Looking down on the propeller shaft. The red blanks facing front are where the coolant header tank connects to the engine. *(Keith Wilson)*

ABOVE Rear of the engine showing the supercharger and carburettor. *(Keith Wilson)*

LEFT Front of engine with propeller shaft, vacuum pump (left) and CSU (right) fitted. *(Keith Wilson)*

Introduction

Mitchell's Spitfire design and Rolls-Royce's Merlin and Griffon engines were, simply, a match made in heaven. Engine capacity increased from 1,100hp to more than 2,300hp over the course of five years. To handle the increase in power during this time, the propeller evolved from a fixed-pitch shaft with two-bladers to one with five-blades. When asked about the engine, the simple but effective description from one veteran was: 'Solid, durable and with plenty of oomph!'

The Rolls-Royce Merlin and Griffon engines were the workhorses of their time and, just as the airframe and weaponry systems evolved during the course of the Second World War, so did the engines and the design of the propellers. Thankfully, there still remain specialist companies who are able to refurbish and service engines to ensure the originality of your Spitfire restoration. The level of refurbishment will be dependent upon the condition of the engine and whether the aircraft is being brought back to flying or static condition. The same applies to propellers, and careful assessments of both are required in order to further facilitate your project.

Removing or sourcing an engine

If your Spitfire comes with an engine that is fitted, then it will require removing. Depending on what pipework there is and the completeness of the oil and coolant systems, the first job will be to drain these systems. You will need a lifting gantry strong enough to bear the weight of the engine, an engine sling, an engine stand and two or three people to operate the gantry and guide the engine out of the engine bearer.

The initial step is to move the gantry over the engine, connect the sling to the lifting eye of the gantry and the three fasteners (legs) to the attachment points on the engine, which are located one on either side to the rear of the engine and one just behind the reduction gear.

The eight bolts securing the engine to the engine bearer are then removed, and all control cables, rods, linkages, fuel pipes, oil and coolant pipes are disconnected. The engine is subsequently lifted clear of the frame, with two of the team stopping the engine from fouling or swinging as the third member operates the gantry to raise the engine.

The engine is then placed on an engine stand and bolted into place, to prevent it from falling off; it can then be transported on this stand to the specialist company that will carry out the overhaul.

If your project did not come with an engine, then you will need to source one suitable

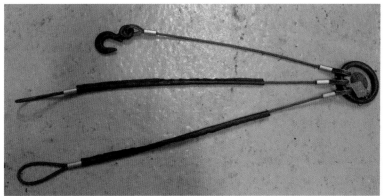

TOP Rear pick-up point for the sling. *(Paul Blackah)*

ABOVE Lifting sling for a Merlin engine. *(Paul Blackah)*

BELOW A tatty Packard 266 waiting to be stripped for spares, or overhauled for use. *(Paul Blackah)*

ABOVE Complete Merlin engine. *(Keith Wilson)*

OPPOSITE Top view of a Griffon engine. *(Paul Blackah)*

BELOW Polished cam cover bearing the famous Rolls-Royce name. *(Keith Wilson)*

for your Spitfire. Surprisingly, auction sites (including ebay) sometimes advertise Merlin and Griffon engines for sale. However, buyer beware, as there are people who will try and sell you something without giving you the full facts and paperwork; it is possible to end up spending £20–30,000 and find that the engine still needs up to £100,000 in restoration costs, or find that it is not viable at all to overhaul. You *must* look at what you are buying in person in order to assess the condition and the amount of work that could be required.

There are other sources, such as companies that buy in engines to overhaul and then sell as complete and finished to your specifications. One such business is Retro Track and Air (see below).

Merlin or Griffon?

This is a fairly straightforward choice, as it simply depends on the mark of Spitfire you are going to restore. The mark that uses the Merlin has a different engine bearer arrangement than the model that uses the Griffon. One is not compatible with the other.

Overhauling the engine

Retro Track and Air is acknowledged as the only Rolls-Royce Plc and RAF-approved Rolls-Royce Merlin and Griffon overhaul facility in the world. Retro's position as a premier overhauler has been hard won and painstakingly maintained for the benefit of its customers and the wider warbird community. Peter Watts tells us more about the company and the process of overhauling an engine.

In addition to entire engine rebuilds, since Retro is a CAA-approved design house and

manufacturing organisation, it carries out new manufacture, repair and/or modification for all the elements of a warbird, including airframe, engine and its systems and propellers.

With engines in mind the following parts are typically in regular new production: camshafts, rockers, cylinder heads, liners, piston rings, bearings etc. Typical repairs include crankcase

main bearing housing rebore/replacement, cylinder head valve seat replacement, valve guide replacement, cylinder head and liner joint facing.

Having completed around 100 Merlin and a dozen Griffon restorations/rebuilds Retro has gathered a wide range of experience on almost all of the models produced by both Rolls-Royce and Packard, from the earliest Battle of Britain spec Merlin IIs right up to the Behemoth high-altitude Griffon 65s. It can be all too easy to forget that operating these types before Retro could be rather hit or miss at times; the limited resources available to some operators was often mitigated with a more plentiful supply and use of new old stock parts. Such a situation no longer exists and the recognition is that the value of parts requires their frugal use, and are not to be wasted.

Retro has amassed a broad spares cache for the full range of types to support it and its customers' ongoing activities. To that end a large stock of parts is carried all the way up to around 20 whole-Rolls-Royce Merlins in varying degrees of readiness; Packard-built Merlins and Griffons are also part of the inventory.

While there are still a few specialist sub-contracting companies operating within the UK that Retro occasionally puts work out to, more often than not, due to the ever shrinking UK manufacturing industry, Retro has had to

ABOVE Cleaned pistons ready for fitting. *(Keith Wilson)*

invest 'deep roots' to undertake the necessary approved works in support of its activities. That's why Retro has in-house NDT, four-axis computer numerical control (CNC) machining, 'original' camshaft grinders and design facilities on site.

It is important to remember that an engine is part of the propulsion system and it is not a stand-alone item. Too often warbird operators have seen the problem as lying with an engine, only to find [the problem] is still there when it returns from the overhaul shop. Oil supply, ancillaries and much more need considering. The more of the whole propulsion system you can look at, the better the outcome.

LEFT A half-set of pistons complete with gudgeon pin. *(Keith Wilson)*

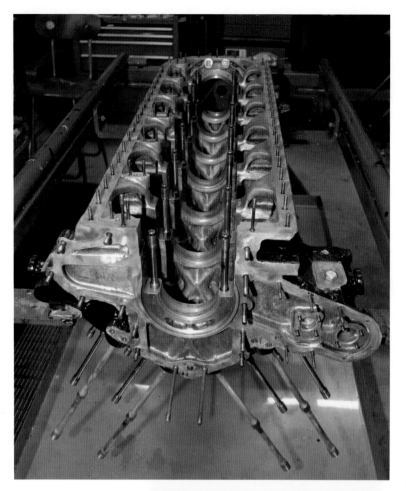

ABOVE Rear end of
the crankcase.
(Keith Wilson)

RIGHT The crankcase
with the conrods
showing and block
studs in place.
(Keith Wilson)

A good example of this holistic approach can be seen in Retro's servicing of oil tanks from most warbirds. The shape of the tanks means that 'gunge' can be lurking in the tight edges, between baffles, just waiting to circulate around the engine and cause difficulties. The tanks are routinely taken apart and cleaned, welded or riveted back together and pressure tested. Oil coolers are dealt with in a different way, but to the same end: a rig is set up to force decarboniser fluid through and this is monitored via filters with the aim being to make the cooler 'as good on the inside as it is on the outside'.

Merlin Mark 66 overhaul process

Upon receipt of an engine, the team at Retro go through a set procedure. The incoming paperwork from the client is compared with what is found after a post-arrival inspection and any differences or omissions are logged and talked over with the owner. From this a work plan is agreed and an engineer assigned – he will 'live' with the job through to test and delivery.

After mounting on a wheeled handling cradle, the engine is stripped to its component parts. All are decarbonised and all paint is removed. Then comes a detailed 'health check' with a vigorous regime of NDT inspections, including magnetic partial and dye-penetrant flaw detection. Retro has the ability to immerse an entire crankcase for such tests. Then comes the many precision dimensional checks on items from the tip of the propeller shaft to the end of the supercharger tail bearing; these will establish the all-important clearances and is essential to the ongoing life and reliability of the engine.

From this, Retro can report to the customer any unserviceabilities or damage, or – in the case of an engine being restored from a non-running state – missing, sub-standard or 'non-spec' components. Armed with this information, any appropriate modifications and/or repair scheme can be arrived at.

Based on the aforementioned inspections a compatible set of matched parts is drawn together to be used in the sub- and final-assembly stages.

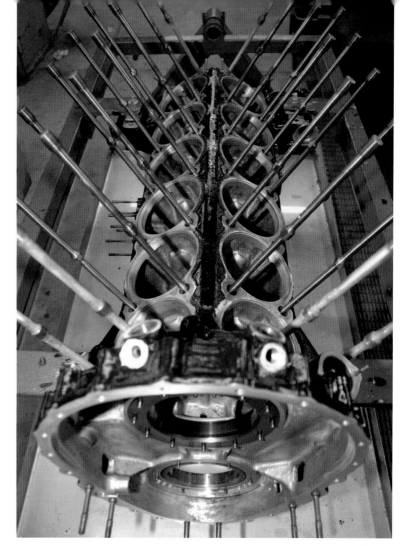

Crankcase, crankshaft and connecting rods are prepared and assembled. The matching of these heavy parts is absolutely critical as the reversing loads are enormous at high rpm settings. The torque to yield tightening of the con rod bolts is perhaps the most crucial task of the assembly process; this is carried out and witnessed by only the most experienced engine builders.

As an example of the possible pitfalls, depending on the following different factors: Packard or Rolls-Royce made bolts and nuts, early or late locating tang, standard or fine threads, engine oil or 'Oildag' lubricant from Messers E.G. Acheson Ltd, Rolls-Royce factory or field method of tightening versus Packard stretch method. Beware those who mix up parts as these engines can go BANG!

In parallel to the above the following sub-assemblies are brought up to a finished stage ready for the big push to complete the engine.

Reduction gearbox assembly requires a mammoth assembly jig to hold back the

ABOVE LEFT The bottom of the engine with the crankshaft exposed. *(Keith Wilson)*

ABOVE The crankcase stripped, with just the block studs fitted. *(Keith Wilson)*

LEFT Crankcase with crankshaft and bearing shells removed. *(Keith Wilson)*

propeller shaft while a torque of up to 1,000ft/lb is applied to the gear pinion bearing nut.

Cylinder banks are put together and pressure tested at 50psi and 70°C; this is no mean feat with 200 seals to contend with. Note also, the cylinder head to liner joint face has a 0.0005in tolerance across its 40in long face.

The wheelcase and supercharger drive with its 11 integrated drives is a very tricky unit to assemble; typical of Rolls-Royce it requires special ground spacers to obtain the correct backlashes and contact patches for the multiple bevel drives.

The fine balancing of the supercharger impeller along with its front and rear clearances makes this a very time-consuming piece of the engine. Rotating at 24 to 28,000rpm it's worth getting it right!

The big push to bring together the major sub-assemblies described is as follows.

With the crankcase assembly mounted in a rotating engine stand, the engine is canted over to 60° to bring one of the cylinder bank joint faces horizontal; the complete bank assembly is mounted on the main studs and lowered using special screw jacks, taking great care to locate all six piston and ring assemblies simultaneously in the cylinders without snapping a piston ring,

ABOVE The engine in the rollover stand. This enables the engine to be worked on at any position. (Keith Wilson)

RIGHT Front end of the crankcase. (Keith Wilson))

FAR RIGHT Block removal tool in place; there are two used. Turn the handles and the block raises. (Paul Blackah)

TOP Engine block lifting tool in position. *(Paul Blackah)*

ABOVE The block being wound down on to its stand.
(Paul Blackah)

BELOW The flame traps, behind which are the engine's fuel
priming pipes. *(Paul Blackah))*

TOP Piston ring clamps guide the piston rings into the cylinder
by making them flush with the piston, thus preventing them
from catching and breaking. *(Paul Blackah)*

ABOVE Exposed pistons with the block removed. *(Paul Blackah)*

BELOW The inlet manifold. *(Paul Blackah)*

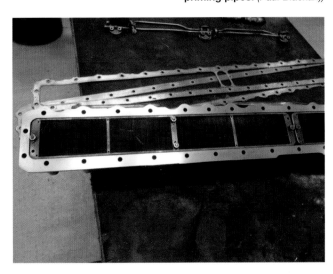

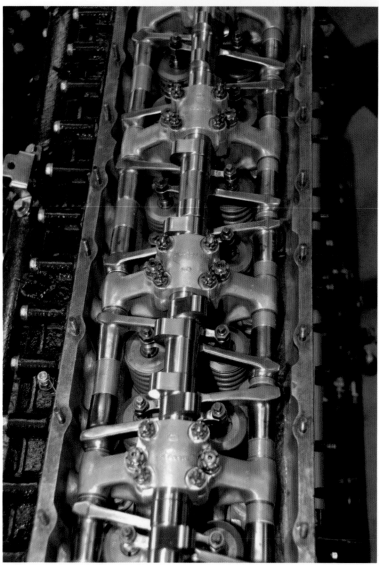

damaging the piston or dislodging a base seal. The other cylinder bank is subsequently fitted in the same manner only with the added difficulty of the first bank obstructing the area. The engine is righted and the flame traps and inlet trunk put into position. The engine is then inverted to fit the lower crankcase, complete with oil pumps. After fitting the unit is righted and attached to a final-assembly stand.

The reduction gearbox assembly is mounted taking great care to align the main reduction gear and pinion gear tooth contact patch; this done the assembly is secured with its dowels and special fitted bolts.

The mounting of the wheel case is next, making sure to check the oil pump drive gear backlash is in situ, followed by the two-speed supercharger drive assembly and the supercharger itself; again numerous clearances and backlash checks are important to get right and can only be done at this advanced state of assembly. Any changes required will mean disassembly and reassembly – very time consuming!

The final stage is to fit the intercooler and its pump assembly, the carburettor and Automatic Boost Control (ABC) unit, including the rather tricky setting up of this interconnected arrangement.

The camshaft assemblies can now be fitted and timed in, along with the magnetos and ignition harnesses and spark plugs. Any errors in the timing or the setting of the carb and ABC can only be found during engine running. This brings us to the post-build testing stage.

Final engine test is carried out on its bespoke dynamometer, to date the only one of its type and a significant investment in time, ingenuity and effort; this has already proved well worthwhile as Retro carries out post-rebuild torque and power curves for all their engines. The reliability of a Retro-restored engine is ensured via the full power and hours of endurance tests it carries out prior to it being installed in to the customer's aircraft for flight testing.

All of this equipment would be worthless if it were not for the human element; the skills and disciplines that Retro's people can call upon are essential. Good practice and attention to detail are the cornerstones of what Retro does.

Ground running

Your aircraft is complete and almost ready to fly. However, before it can take to the air, the engine has to be ground run to monitor engine performance levels such as oil temperatures, coolant temperatures, correct boost at the right rpm and also to make sure there are no leaks – for example within the oil, coolant and fuel systems – and that the engine isn't running too 'rich' or too 'lean'.

At RAF BBMF an initial engine run, with fire cover, takes place in order to check that there are no major fuel or oil leaks that could cause an immediate fire. Cover is provided by a fire

engine stationed close to the aircraft. Ground running with fire cover is generally common practice at the larger airfields with their own full-time fire service.

Ground runs are usually carried out by the ground engineers following procedures as set down in the MP146. The procedure, taken directly from the MP146 is as follows:

Firstly, ensure that the aircraft has sufficient fuel to carry out the ground run. This may seem an obvious statement, but it has been known for engineers to try and start an engine with no fuel in the tank and then spend subsequent hours trying to establish why the engine won't start!

Secure the aircraft to the ground to prevent movement; this is done by chocking the aircraft,

placing a strap over the rear of the fuselage across frames 18/19 and securing said strap to a metal ring set in concrete. Two ropes are then run from the metal ring to the chocks, which stops the aircraft moving forward and tipping on its nose.

Ensure that a fire extinguisher and a ground external power supply trolley are readily available. The trolley is used if the aircraft batteries are not fitted in order to supply electrical power.

Take off the pitot cover and walk around the aircraft making certain that all intakes are free from obstruction and that any control locks are removed.

On entering the cockpit, switch on the electrical power, confirming a minimum of 12v. Check that the undercarriage lever is selected DOWN and indicates DOWN. When the engine starts up, the selector should automatically click into IDLE. This tells the person running the engine that the hydraulic pump is supplying pressure. The control column is then pulled backwards and secured with the seat's safety harness. (This ensures that the person running the engine does not have to worry about keeping the stick pulled back, thus keeping his hands free to operate the engine controls and to complete the check sheet.)

The brakes are then set to ON and locked in position and the engine is ready to be started.

The propeller control lever is pushed fully forward, the radiator shutters are opened and the throttle lever is moved forward approximately half an inch. A static reading is noted from the boost gauge. The start isolate switch is set to ON along with the fuel cock lever, and the priming pump is then operated four or five times in order to prime the engine with fuel. Magneto switches are set to ON followed by simultaneously pressing the starter button and the booster coil button until the engine is running steadily. Switch off the start isolate switch and make certain that the oil pressure gauge is indicating the oil pressure.

The engine now needs to be warmed up and this is achieved by maintaining a steady 1,000rpm until the engine coolant temperature is at least 40°C, oil temperature is not less than 15°C and the oil pressure is above 45lb psi.

After the above pressures and temperatures

have been reached, the throttle lever should be moved to obtain 1,200rpm. At this rpm the magnetos are tested; the number 1 switch is set to OFF and the engine rpm should not drop by more than 100rpm. The number 1 switch is then set to ON and the procedure is then repeated with the number 2 switch. This check ensures that both magnetos are operating while the engine is running. If the rpm drop is over 100rpm, on either side, then the fault needs to be investigated. The problem could be anything from a fouled spark plug, insulation on the wiring of the plugs breaking down, or ultimately a magneto that is beginning to fail. This test is also carried out prior to take-off and if the mag drop is excessive, over the limits, the aircraft should not fly.

The next procedure is to turn both magneto switches off and check that a dead cut occurs (the engine stops momentarily). This means that both magnetos cease correctly and that one does not remain 'live'. This, if not monitored, can result in the engine firing again when it is supposedly switched off. If someone was turning the prop, by hand, when the engine fired unexpectedly under these circumstances it could result in a fatality or serious injury. Hence the expression, 'always treat a propeller as "live"'.

The next stage of the engine run is to set ZERO boost and exercise the prop by moving the propeller speed control lever from MIN to MAX and ensure that the rpm increases to 1,650–1,800, at the minimum, again checking the magnetos at this rpm to make certain they are working correctly. A small rpm drop up to 100rpm is permitted; anything over 100 rpm means that the engine should be shut down and plugs inspected for fouling, oiled up and not firing. A continuity check should be carried out on the plug leads themselves to make sure they are not breaking down internally, thus giving intermittent power to the spark plug, and finally the magnetos' points should be examined for cleanliness and the correct gap. If a large mag drop is ignored it could result in the engine misfiring and ultimately losing power, which could mean the loss of the aircraft and possibly the pilot also.

The next check is to move the prop lever to coarse pitch, which should give 2,300rpm. Open the throttle by 1lb boost and ensure that the boost and the rpm are maintained. Close the throttle by 1lb boost and, again, check that it keeps up boost and rpm. Reset the prop lever to fine pitch and next set plus 9 boost, carry out another magneto drop, ensure that you obtain maximum rpm of 2,950 and that the maximum boost does not exceed +12. The +12 is a BBMF setting; some Merlins can be boosted to +18, a combat rating. The +12 sees that the engine does not become over boosted and therefore stress to the engine is kept at a minimum for less wear and tear.

During the above runs the oil temperature should not go beyond 90°C, the coolant temperature must not be more than 120°C and the oil pressure should be above the minimum 30lb psi.

The rpm is then reduced to 600–650rpm and the slow-running cut-off is operated. The engine should stop, the ignition switches are shut off and the fuel cock is set to OFF. This completes the engine ground run, and if all your figures are obtained and within limits then the engine is serviceable.

Each time an engine is ground run, be it for the first few times after a refurbish or after a snag, such as when a leak has been corrected, the above procedure is followed and a check list filled in, which includes the engine number, reason for test and person(s) conducting the test, and at the side of the expected readings there are spaces to record what is actually occurring during the test. The results will determine the next course of action; for example, whether there are certain parts of the engine that are not functioning correctly and need inspecting.

Following a successful initial ground run further tests will be carried out to assess the functions of various components:

Low power

This ground run will check that the engine idle rpm is correctly set and that oil pressure and coolant temperature are within limits. After these runs the coolant system and oil system pipework/radiators and oil cooler are checked for leaks. Any 'weeping' joints are tightened as the rubber hoses are bedding in on to the pipework.

RAF BBMF MERLIN ENGINE GROUND RUNNING SHEET (MAX POWER)	
Before start	
Pneumatic pressure	Minimum 150psi
Brake pressure L and R	Minimum 90psi on both sides
Fuel pressure light	ON
Generator light	ON
Voltage indicated	24v minimum
After start	
Oil pressure	Minimum 50psi
Generator light	OFF
Fuel pressure light	OFF
Voltmeter	28.5v maximum
Flaps	Operate
Mag drop L and R	100rpm max (aircrew 150rpm max)
Mag dead cut	Momentarily both off and restore
Pneumatic pressure	Build up to 300psi
Oil temperature	Ensure above 15°C for opening up (80° max)
Radiator temperature	40°C for opening up (100° max)
At 'Zero' boost	
Exercise prop	(X3)
Min governed rpm	1,650–1,800rpm
Mag drop L and R	100rpm max (aircrew 150rpm max)
Set 2,500rpm	
Prop lever to coarse pitch	Set 2,300rpm
Open throttle by 1lb boost	Ensure maintains boost and rpm
Close throttle by 1lb boost	Ensure maintains boost and rpm
Prop lever	Set to fine pitch
Set +9 boost	
Mag drop +9 Boost (L and R)	100rpm max (aircrew 150 max rpm)
At full throttle	
Max rpm	Ensure max 2,950rpm
Max boost	Do not exceed +12
Set 'Zero' boost and record reference rpm	
Set 1,000rpm	
rpm	Reduce rapidly to min
Minimum rpm	600–650rpm
Set 1,000rpm	
SRCO	Ensure slightly rev rise

High power

This run ensures that the CSU (constant speed unit) is set up correctly to make certain the engine gets maximum rpm and that the propeller is exercised throughout its range. It also confirms that the engine boost is set to its running limits. It may take several engine runs to establish the correct settings. After this run all pipework is checked again.

BELOW The brass erosion strip and wood grain are exposed with the paint stripped off the blades.
(Paul Blackah)

Removing or sourcing a propeller

If your project comes with a propeller, and it is still fitted, then it will need to be removed from the aircraft, and this is achieved by first detaching the spinner (again if fitted), then taking off the propeller's piston assembly, complete with oil tube; the propeller nut is then undone and the propeller will, hopefully, be able to be lifted away.

If the propeller is complete with blades, two lifting slings are required with a lifting gantry to raise the prop assembly. If there are no blades – for example they have been cut and only the hub remains – two or three people should be able to hoist this part off.

Once removed, the propeller assembly will need overhauling back to airworthy condition.

Where to have it overhauled

Skycraft Services Ltd are the leading company for Spitfire propeller overhauls and have been since 1990. Michael Barnett, head of the company, tells us a little about the business and the process of refurbishment.

Skycraft was established in 1987 to support Hoffmann GmbH & Co KG (who manufacture traditional wooden laminated blades) in developing the UK market, and the warbird sector was an important and prestigious part of the plan. GE Dowty, who were the wartime manufacturers of propeller assemblies, have taken a very responsible approach to the continued support of the Rotol Airscrew Propeller and this world-class support has indirectly enabled Sptifires to continue to fly with the knowledge the propeller is by and large unaffected by age.

In the early 1980s the CAA Propulsion Department, represented by the late Jeff Thomasson, agreed that Dowty, Hoffmann and Skycraft should cooperate in the development and supply of new propeller blades, and this would be the basis of continued airworthiness for the vintage Rotol propeller. As Dowty were moving into carbon-fibre composite production for their modern propellers, Hoffmann provided the manufacturing capability, as their business is primarily based on traditional wood laminated blades. Their release to service procedure

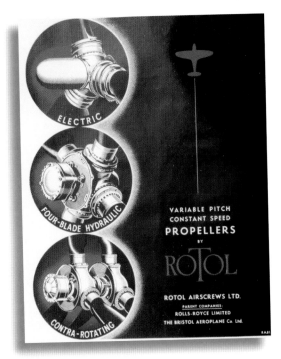

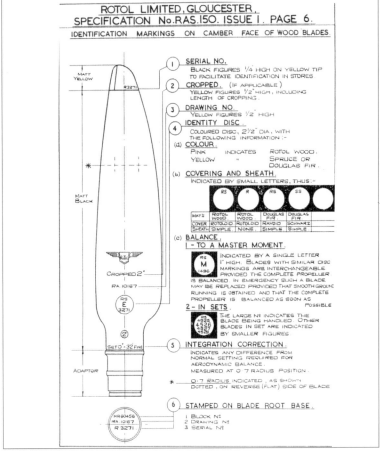

called 'authentication' being that new blades manufactured by Hoffmann are inspected and released by Dowty, and due to the high costs of development Dowty do not support the use of replacement blades manufactured by any other company than Hoffmann.

ABOVE LEFT An advertisement from later in the war for Dowty Rotol propellers.

ABOVE Propeller blade information on identification markings.

LEFT Propeller assembly bench.

maintenance and operational level, are specified in Dowty Service Bulletin 61-1061 Rev 1 and 61-1113. Today there is a range of replacement blades manufactured by Hoffmann and sold by Skycraft, which form the basis of operation of the vintage Rotol propellers in use worldwide in the three-, four- and five-blade configurations.

There are three types of propellers: the three-blade propellers (RX5/RS5 series) are non-standardised, which means each type is different; for example, the arrangement for the hold-down nut differs and there are no common parts. The three-blade propeller dates back to the late 1930s and it is fascinating that one of the contracts Rotol were chasing was to be the supplier for the propeller of the 'new' Messerschmitt 109 aircraft! In terms of standardisation and continuity of engineering records the four- and five-blade propellers are easier to maintain and are generally more robust products, having had the benefit of several years of continued development. It is thought that the five-blade propeller (R14/R19 series) continued in production until the late 1950s.

The authentication process, after Hoffmann manufacture, involves inspection of aerofoil alignments, check of structural integrity, measurement of natural frequencies and determination of aerodynamic correction factors. In this way a Rotol propeller, fitted with replacement Hoffmann blades, is a fully supported, certified product, which conforms to laid-down requirements, which, at the

From a Chief Technician's perspective, a clear distinction of the work scope needs to be made when referring to any aspect of

maintenance of these propellers. There are three categories: rebuild of an original propeller, which has remained unused since the war; overhaul of a propeller, which has not been previously seen by Skycraft (eg US-operated aircraft); and overhaul of a previously assembled Skycraft propeller. Very simply, servicing a propeller takes about 250 hours. The combined requirements mean that we have about ten propellers undergoing maintenance most of the time.

With regards to cost, it's difficult to quote an exact figure as there are many variables to factor in. An overhaul can be £15,000 and a major rebuild £100,000, with all sorts of options in between; for instance, repair of a propeller after a ground strike when new blades are required.

Where spares are concerned, initially there were sources of NOS (non-operational spares), but with the level of activity these have long since been used up. Today we manufacture all new parts and carry an extensive stock of the commonly used replacement parts. The investment in this manufacturing capability has been significant and all new parts are made to conform exactly to the original drawings.

Fortunately, 300 Spitfires have survived; many complete as exhibits in aircraft museums around the world. With the extraordinary level

of interest in the Spitfire today as the instantly recognisable iconic fighter of the Second World War, restoration to airworthy condition is a realistic proposition given a sizeable investment, as explained in other chapters of this Manual. Specialist organisations, such as Historic Flying Limited and Airframe Assemblies Limited, have invested in the resources necessary to repair and restore the aircraft to immaculate flying condition, which is resulting in more of the survivors being restored to flight.

Spitfire Mark Is were initially fitted with a Watts fixed pitch two-blade propeller, and later an American Hamilton Standard variable pitch three-blade propeller manufactured under licence by the de Havilland Aircraft Company. At this time Rotol Airscrews Limited was formed after the Ministry of Supply, conscious of the threat of war with Germany, realised it would be in the national interest to concentrate the talent of Rolls-Royce and the Bristol Aeroplane Company into a single airscrew organisation. The merger, whose name was a contraction of 'ROlls-Royce and BrisTOL', worked well despite previous rivalry, and by combining their propeller activities established a firm capable of technical development of the Hele-Shaw & Beacham concepts for variable pitch propellers

RIGHT Three-blade propeller with piston assembly fitted.
(Paul Blackah)

with hydraulic control to match the rapid development of aircraft engines.

Rotol airscrews were given designations that in part defined the SBAC (Society of British Aircraft Constructors) splined shafts to which they fitted and, for example, one of the first production propellers, Rotol R4/1 (SBAC No 4 spline), was for a three-blade propeller for the Bristol Blenheim (of which 500 were subsequently ordered by the Air Ministry). The first Rotol airscrew for a Spitfire was RX5/1 for a Mark II aircraft with a Rolls-Royce Merlin XII engine, and this utilised magnesium alloy as opposed to wood blades because of the difficulty being experienced in attaching wood blades to metal ferrules for fitment to the propeller hub. Rotol gave attention to resolving the blade fixing problems with the introduction of compressed resin-bonded composite wood, so that the considerations of weight, battle damage repair, flexible manufacturing, etc could be worked to advantage. Additionally, one important feature, which only became apparent during the war, was the ability of wooden blades to shatter during an accident without causing serious damage to the engine, its mounting, or the propeller hub itself. It was known that Germany was more advanced in the manufacture of blades for high-performance aircraft using composite wood, and through post-war cooperation, experimental blades were made by Rotol under licence from the German Heine and Schwartz propeller manufacturers.

With war imminent and the rapid advancement in blade design and production, the Air Ministry placed an order with Rotol for 5,000 airscrews by the beginning of 1939. As the Spitfire developed and production increased, the Rotol three-blade propeller became the standard fitment. Rotol used three-blade designs involving different layouts made of the high British manufactured density woods: Jablo, Jicwood and Hydulignum. In addition to the Rotol site, production of blades was also undertaken at the dispersed sites of The Airscrew Company, Hordern-Richmond Aircraft Ltd and F. Hills & Sons Ltd. By the close of the Second World War, Rotol had produced over 100,000 airscrews in varying configurations for over 60 different training, fighter and bomber aircraft.

To explain in part what is involved in Rotol propeller overhaul to meet today's airworthiness regulations, we will consider the requirements for an aircraft that has been on display in a museum since retirement from service. The Spitfire Mark IX was produced in the greatest numbers, with a Rotol R12/4F5/4 propeller, and it is this constant-speed four-blade propeller with wood blades that is the subject of the following description.

Restoring a Rotol R12/4F5/4 propeller

The large spinner assembly on the propeller protects the hub components and it is unusual to find a Rotol propeller on a museum aircraft to be disturbed, or robbed of parts. Of course, maintenance documentation is desirable, but unlikely to have survived the ravages of time, and so the overhaul of the propeller must go beyond routine maintenance in order to scrutinise all the elements. At the BBMF one of our experienced engineers will be able to determine whether the propeller has been dismantled previously or whether it is extant from its last operational use.

The pitch change system has to be taken apart to enable the propeller to be removed from the Merlin output shaft. The actuating eye bolts are disconnected and the cylinder cover removed, and the engine oil in the cylinder is drained. Blade pitch change is achieved with hydraulic pressure to a moving cylinder against a stationary piston, which is connected to the engine constant-speed unit via oil tubes through the output shaft. The piston is detached, followed by the cylinder and the inner and outer oil tubes. Removal of these groups gives access to the hold-down nut, which is a tight fit and once taken off, together with the front cone, allows the propeller assembly to be displaced forward with lifting equipment. The propeller is mounted between cones front and back on the output shaft, and examination for fretting on all the cone surfaces is important.

With the propeller installed horizontally on a rig, preparation is made for blade removal by dismantling the various cover and lock plates. To counteract the flying loads and centrifugal force from the blade, large ball or taper roller bearings are used on the blade root. The bearing preloads have to be freed as the raceways are expanded to form a tight fit

BELOW The locking
rings that attach the
blade into the hub.
(Paul Blackah)

in the hub blade port. A special tool is used to
hold the operating link and then spanners are
installed to the blade root preload nut to release
the torque. One of the problems with heavily
loaded bearings if the propeller has not been
in regular use is that the raceways suffer from
crevice corrosion. This causes notchy operation
and a high break torque, which is unacceptable,
and during overhaul it may be necessary to
replace the bearing raceways – a complex task.

When a blade is removed from the hub it is
placed in a large clamping fixture so that the
operating pins, actuating plates, retaining nuts
and bearings can be taken off. The hub, which
at this stage is stripped of all major groups, is a
forged shell with a driving centre installed with
interference fit bolts in the attachment flanges.
The hub and driving centre must be split to
reveal the mating flange faces and facilitate
detailed inspection of the hub.

The propeller dismantling process is
completed by taking apart all the sub-
assemblies so that every part can be serviced
individually– (a Rotol R12/4F5/4 propeller
comprises about 800 parts). The smaller
items are replaced at overhaul and major
components subjected to a series of processes
to ascertain and re-establish their condition. All
parts are cleaned and stripped of the previous
surface finish for inspection and dimensional
checks. The major components are crack
tested using dye penetrant, magnetic particle
and eddy current methods, as required. If
parts are worn it may be possible to repair
to a Rotol salvage scheme. Maintenance
documentation for the Rotol propeller
was produced as Rotol Publications (the
manufacturer's manuals) and also by the Air
Ministry in the form of air publications (which are
more comprehensive). For the Rotol R12/4F5/4
propeller the manuals are Rotol Publication 504
(1946) and Air Publication AP1538E (1944).
With such large-scale adoption of the Rotol
propeller during the Second World War, the Air
Publication series was very detailed and was
structured in volumes covering all aspects of
the propeller system.

When rework and inspection of all parts has
been completed, new surface treatments are
applied using the original specifications, thereby
maintaining complete authenticity. For example,
a surface protection popular with Rotol was
a form of phosphating using the proprietary
Parco-Lubrite solution, Specification No
RAS100, which produces a thin crystalline film
of phosphates of iron in the surface of steel that
readily absorbs oil to provide good corrosion
protection while minimising fretting and galling
between mating surfaces. This is the coating
that provides the characteristic matt black finish
of many Rotol propeller parts.

From experience it is known that Rotol propeller blades constructed 70 years ago are unlikely to be serviceable, and checks of the moisture content of the timber, together with X-rays of the structure to look for voids, and aerofoil alignment measurements, are likely to confirm this. The common problem is the drying out of the wood resulting in cracking, particularly at the blade root, or failure of the glued laminates. There are probably only one or two propellers in use today that have original Rotol blades and these are fitted to Spitfires which have been in near continuous use.

The procedures adopted for provision of replacement propeller blades were devised by the late Jeff Thomasson in his role as a CAA Powerplant Surveyor in the early 1980s. A series of replacement blades have been developed by the German propeller manufacturer Hoffmann GmbH & Co KG, covering all Spitfire Rotol propeller types. These authentic blades are approved by GE Dowty and backed by extensive development, testing and evaluation, including spinning tower tests. One of the findings from development was that the harmonics of the blades are critical and so it is necessary to maintain flexural and torsional frequencies between specified limits to avoid operation of the propeller near harmonic flutter. In 1938 Rotol developed a 'top secret' blade integration machine called Q-set that determines the aerodynamic balance to provide an integration correction factor, which when applied to the blade angle setting ensures smooth running of the propeller. The only surviving integration machine is in the care of Skycraft and is used regularly to implement Rotol Specification No RAS 140.

Given the exacting attention to detail that is given to Spitfire wartime colour schemes today, the same treatment must also be accorded to the propeller, where blade markings have great significance. The marking scheme is defined in the Rotol documentation, such as Rotol Specification No RAS 150, and an important aspect of original marking is the application of the attractive Rotol trademark – the 'wings' logo.

Some of the other essential quality control activities, which are part of a propeller overhaul, include assessment of build

standard, modification status and assimilation of the compatibility of all parts to be used for the rebuild. Skycraft has a wide-ranging manufacturing capability, and to support its worldwide customer base maintains a large stock of Rotol parts. The reassembly process relies heavily on special equipment, strict adherence to procedure, attention to the detail of limits fits and clearances, and several days of uninterrupted work by two skilled engineers!

The GE Dowty/Hoffmann/Skycraft cooperation has worked well and this has allowed progressive improvement in the condition of the propellers in use, and propeller reconstructions for newly restored aircraft to an immaculate and completely authentic standard. It must be said the proper maintenance of Rotol propellers could not have reached today's standards without the world-class technical and continued airworthiness support from GE Dowty for what is now one of their heritage propellers, and in respect of the blades a committed policy of authentication which means that all replacement Hoffmann blades are inspected and released by GE Dowty with the sure knowledge they comply with the design standard and the resultant Rotol propeller conforms to the original specifications.

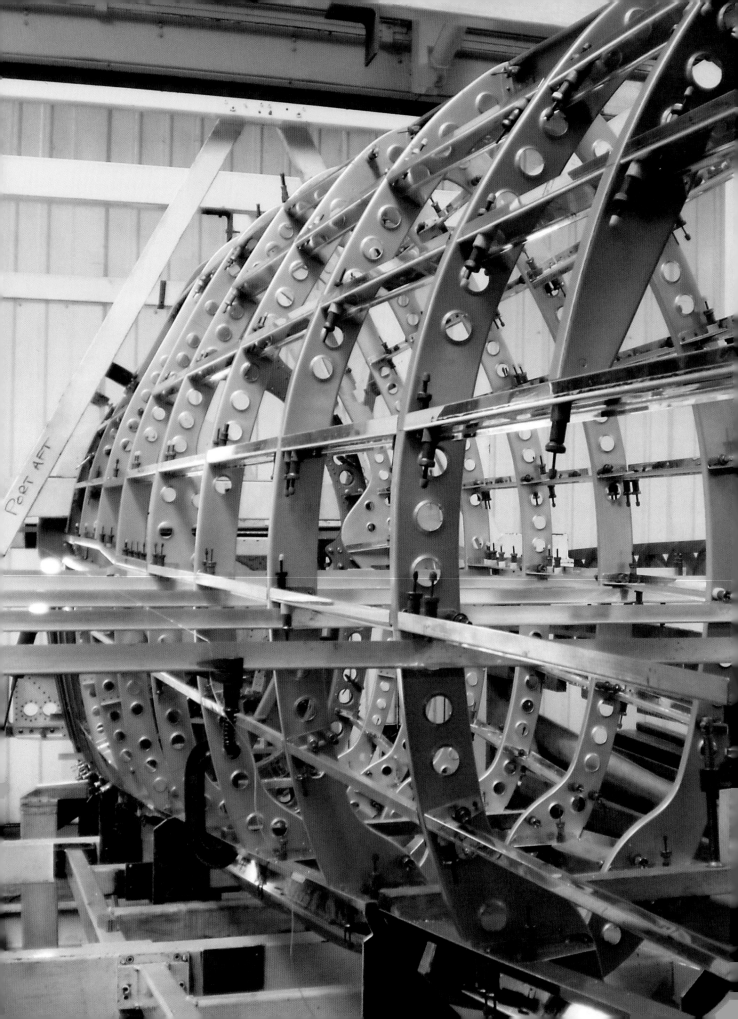

Chapter Five

Airframe

During the Second World War Mitchell's original design was repeatedly modified and improved. Factories worked overtime to make these changes but the Germans were doing the same with their Bf109s and Fw190s. Keeping one step ahead of the opposition eventually saw 24 marks of Spitfire and 7 marks of Seafire produced. Potential restorers today will find certain marks easier to work with and for sourcing spares. Finding earlier marks of Spitfires for restoration is virtually impossible, which makes those already flying highly sought after.

OPPOSITE Fuselage frames and intercostals gripped in place. Note that neither the frames nor the intercostals are drilled yet for the skins to be fitted. Once drilled, they will require dimpling. *(Airframe Assemblies)*

RIGHT Assembled frames waiting to be positioned in the jig. *(VMI Engineering)*

BELOW Frame 5 assembled and placed in the jig. *(VMI Engineering)*

Restoring the fuselage

After the strip down and inspection of the fuselage components and any parts that need replacing or refurbishing have been acquired, the next step is to assemble the fuselage in its entirety. This is where the fuselage jig comes into its own.

The jig itself is already pre-built with all the correct datums in place, so it will give you the pick-up points for frame 5, frame 19 and the lower and middle datum longerons. This enables you to lay in the components in their correct position, knowing that your fuselage will be the correct length, width and height.

To begin assembly, position frame 5 into the jig and bolt it into place. Next, offer up the lower datum longerons, followed by the mid-datum longerons, which should clamped in place to prevent movement and distortion. If these longerons are the originals then all the holes for all the frames will already be present, which, when fitting each frame from frame 6 to frame 19, will make the job easier. If, however, they are replacements then all the holes will need to be drilled in the correct positions for each frame. This, in itself, is no simple task as accuracy is obviously essential. Incorrect positioning of the frame could mean that your skin, if already drilled, might not line up with the frame.

After making sure that all the frames/ longerons are drilled, each item is removed and any swarf (metal shavings) is cleaned off. The frames and longerons are then painted and reassembled ready for riveting. On assembly the mating surfaces are coated with a jointing compound (JC5A), which protects these surfaces from corrosion. Any excess should be wiped away prior to riveting. Each frame from frame 6 to frame 19 is riveted in place. The top longeron from frame 11 to frame 19 is then also fitted and riveted in position.

RIGHT **Looking back from frame 11, the two tie-wrapped units on frame 11 hold the seat in place.** *(VMI Engineering)*

ABOVE Fuselage frames with a top longeron in place. *(VMI Engineering)*

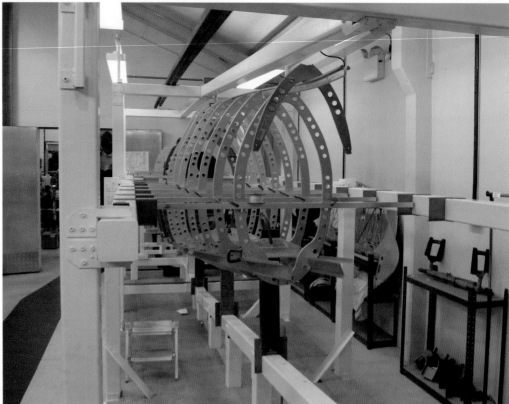

RIGHT This picture gives you an idea on how big and sturdy the fuselage jig is. *(VMI Engineering)*

SPITFIRE RESTORATION MANUAL

ABOVE Frame 11 (green) detail. *(Airframe Assemblies)*

LEFT Frames gripped to the longerons. The green frame is frame 11. *(Airframe Assemblies)*

RIGHT Skins are drilled and gripped into position using skin pins. *(Airframe Assemblies)*

BELOW Fuselage frames and intercostals, held ready for riveting. *(Airframe Assemblies)*

All the intercostals and their attachment brackets are connected next. These join the frames together, forming a skeletal structure to which the skins can be attached. Again, if original they will simply require fitting and if new will need to have the holes drilled and dimpled or countersunk. The fuselage is then ready to accept the skins.

If new skins are called for the old ones can be used as a pattern; however, this is dependent on condition. If the condition of the original skin is too poor, then the holes for the skin are picked up from the holes in the framework, by placing the new skin over the frames and then drilling through, gripping it in place while the process is carried out. If the old skin can be used as a pattern the new skin would be placed over the old one and all the holes picked up, again by drilling through one skin to the other while holding the two skins together using gripper pins (skin pins) to prevent movement.

Once the skins have been drilled all the holes need deburring, which basically means you are removing any sharp edges around the hole. Next, depending on what mark of Spitfire you have, you either do nothing to the holes on the

ABOVE Fuselage skins being riveted in place. *(Airframe Assemblies)*

BELOW Frames 6, 7 and 8 in their locations. *(Airframe Assemblies)*

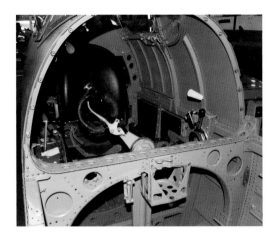

FAR LEFT Looking into the cockpit area at frame 8. *(Airframe Assemblies)*

LEFT Windscreen and canopy in place. *(Airframe Assemblies)*

skin or you countersink the holes or dimple the holes. Counter-sinking is done using a tool that removes material from the metal, to allow you to fit a flush rivet. The angle of the countersink is usually one of three angles: 90, 100 or 120°. Dimpling is carried out when the skin is too thin to countersink and is done either by hand or by machine. Each hole is placed under a mandrel, which is shaped to either 100° or 120° (the shape of the rivet) and the machine then squeezes the mandrel into a corresponding female die. This is done for every hole and, as you can imagine, there are quite a few to be done. The skin then gives the appearance of being countersunk, but on the back of the skin it is dimpled. If the skin is dimpled the frames also require this process to allow the skin to fit flush up against the frame.

Once drilled the skins are painted prior to assembly and are gripped into position, having also had the mating surfaces of the frame

to skin applied with jointing compound. The riveting can begin once both parts are in place.

Each skin in turn follows this procedure and, after days of riveting, your fuselage will be complete. During the skin fitment process, some electrical wiring will need to be put in place, as it is routed down the inside of the lower datum longeron. This should be done before the skins go on otherwise you will not have access. Other items, such as anchor nuts and cable fairleads, are also fitted.

OPPOSITE Inside RW382's fuselage: you can see the many intercostals that join the frames. *(Airframe Assemblies)*

RIVET SPECIFICATIONS

Snap head rivet (domed)	SP80
Mush head rivet	SP85
Countersunk 100° rivet	SP71
Countersunk 120°	AS2229
Countersunk 90°	AS2230

LEFT RW382's fuselage from the left-hand side. The cut-out in the fuselage behind the windscreen is for the cockpit door. *(Airframe Assemblies)*

Fin unit, tailplanes and ailerons

The same process that is carried out on the fuselage is also performed on the fin unit, tailplanes and ailerons. A purpose-built jig for each part is required, again to ensure correct dimensions are achieved and items are not built with a twist or distortion.

Airframe Assemblies, based on the Isle of Wight, are a company specialising in the refurbishment of all the major airframe components of the Spitfire; for example, the fuselage, wings, panels, fin unit and cowlings. Steve Vizard, owner of the company, explains to us a little about Airframe Assemblies, what they do and the restraints they work within:

The Spitfire restoration industry began in the late 1970s – the movement was in its infancy at this stage, and slowly developed over the next few years as Spitfire wrecks/projects began to appear and attract the first raft of owners. Up to this point the primary task had been to repair rather than replace items, but with the advent of more aircraft in poorer condition and up for rebuild, the repair work became hard to achieve if the aircraft was going to stand up to official scrutiny. Up to the early 1980s, most rebuilds had not attracted a great attention from the CAA, as there was not then the need for the involvement we have today.

At that time I don't think anyone could foresee that the disparate individuals and early workshops would evolve into the extremely professional and commercial enterprises that exist in 2013. Close monitoring and substantial regulation from the CAA has followed, but those companies that today restore these classic icons are all fully approved and frequently inspected by the Authority.

Airframe Assemblies was one of these companies that started to restore and provide replacement parts for the Spitfires in the mid-1980s and was officially incorporated into the system in 1986.

The background interest in the Battle of Britain, and the collecting of the relics of this period, had initially led to having made contact with Aero Vintage in Hastings, and ultimately then to working there on a semi-voluntary basis, and I should give mention to Steve Atkins and Guy Black at this point.

As it became more apparent that there was an opportunity to start a business centred more on the airframe components (than to be involved in systems and fitting out), it also became apparent that the skill base necessary for these aspects of Spitfire rebuilding were only readily available on the South Coast and in the Isle of Wight/Portsmouth/Bournemouth area where there was (and still is) a comparatively strong aerospace sector.

With a part-time staff of two, the first job was to rebuild the fin/rudder and elevator of a Mark XVIII Spitfire, and then we managed to gain some orders from an often unsung pioneer of serious Spitfire restorations – Charles Church.

At this juncture AA was actually formed, and moved into a small modern industrial unit in Sandown on the Isle of Wight.

The order book gradually increased and several more moves followed, and we are currently located on Sandown airfield in a brand new 15,000sq ft hangar with a staff of 24.

Over the 26 years that AA have been in

BELOW Fuselage frames with datum longerons and many of the intercostals in position. *(Airframe Assemblies)*

existence, the company has produced parts of just about every airworthy Spitfire, from minor detail items, to complete fuselage, tail and wing assemblies, and all associated airframe parts.

During this period, we have also worked on almost 50 other types (not all vintage or warbird), including major rebuilds on the only genuine airworthy Messerschmitt 109E, and all the major Hawker aircraft.

Currently AA holds full CAA manufacturing supplier approvals, and also those applicable to restoration/rebuilds in the permit to fly category and is shortly to be issued with the latest approval (A8-21) that the CAA has now deemed appropriate. All a far cry from the early 1980s!

Over the years, the company has built up the most comprehensive library of drawings and technical publications that it is possible to have, that have survived as original copies.

We do have facilities to produce drawings where these originals do not exist, and these are then approved and signed for by our design consultant – all of which is an absolute requirement as an approved company.

The appropriate assembly jigs, and all the required tooling – comprising press blocks, stretch form tools, wheeling horses, lay up boards, templates and so forth, have all been produced to enable AA to make just about any detail part, major or assembly, for all marks of Spitfire – at least up to the 20 series.

The level of interest in Spitfires is stronger today than it has ever been, with more potential owners realising what a positive investment a Spitfire currently is, which has to be a serious consideration in the present climate. Although most customers are extremely passionate about the aircraft, and the history and aura that surround them, the decision to undertake a rebuild/restoration is a major one that consumes a substantial sum of money, and about three years of involvement. It has to be gratifying to know that the gap between the cost and the value of the aircraft is a positive one. Many of those who invest in their passions and hobbies that involve other types of aircraft, classic cars and so forth spend more than the end result is worth – happily the Spitfire transcends this level and it does broaden its appeal.

After all, we all want to see as many Spitfires as possible back in the air, and despite

ABOVE RW382's fuselage nearing completion at Airframe Assemblies. *(Airframe Assemblies)*

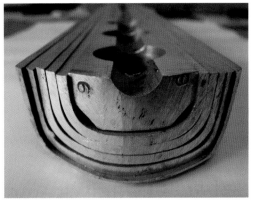

LEFT Cross section showing how the main spar is constructed. *(Paul Blackah)*

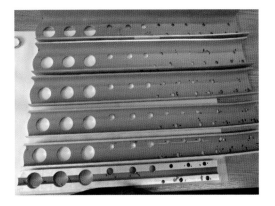

LEFT Section of the main spar showing the six separate layers. *(Paul Blackah)*

all the restorations carried out over the last 30 years, we are still hardly at 50–55 aircraft airworthy worldwide.

To recreate the engineering and production methods of the 1930s does present a set of challenges that, on the surface, one would think should be easy to apply 2014 techniques to – but generally this is a misconception.

When Spitfires were in full production, it should be remembered that only ten years before, aircraft had been predominately of tubular steel/wood and fabric construction, and the all-aluminium monocoque of a Spitfire represented a technological leap forward in the way components were made.

Sheet-metal-formed parts were made on large stretching machines and rubber die presses. Forgings were commonplace as the standard way to produce multiples of brackets and embedded fittings – a process that today is fed into a complex CNC machining centre and uses a solid billet to mill or turn the component.

Today, obviously, we do not make enough batches of machined fittings for Spitfires to warrant boxes of parts being produced in this manner – and too much 'stock' is not commercially viable.

Although upon occasion CNC (Computer Numerical Control) centres are used, the majority of parts are made on manual machines, as we usually only need a one-off for a particular restoration.

This change of production method does, however, give rise to another issue – that of a deviation from the original manufacturing process. This has to be dealt with by the design process investigating any possible strength and loading issues, and raising the necessary paperwork to approve each individual part.

This is an absolute necessity nowadays, and if one thing has changed markedly since the 1930s it is the level and complexity of the paperwork, which now has to substantiate everything that we do on an official CAA level according to our current approvals, and which allows us to officially release all parts.

The paperwork level required for producing parts for Spitfires is now approaching the commercial standard for the modern aerospace industry, which, although a good discipline to uphold, can be very difficult when dealing with 70-year-old production and material issues.

From the moment an order is received, every component has its own work pack which follows every process, material treatment, tooling/work method, from a raw piece of

RIGHT The complete fuselage of RW382.
(Airframe Assemblies)

material from the stores through to a completed and finished item, inspected and released.

Although we can produce parts using similar or identical methods to the Supermarine factory, one of the biggest areas of official contention is materials. It may be that the basic aluminium sheet, H/T carbon steels, and bars/billets are *almost* identical to their 1930s counterparts; however, officialdom and bureaucracy have decreed that they are, of course, actually different – which is technically accurate as the call-up and specifications have altered over the years.

Due to the foregoing, AA have amassed a large amount of documentary and technical information concerning all the common usage aircraft materials of the 1930s (including German and American), and based upon published data from that era, following direct lineage to the present day, AA have, after several years of investment, managed to produce a materials register which has now become an approved document and allows us to use the listed specifications without constant referral to our design consultant – although of course all so-called substitutions still have to be annotated and drawn!

So although it is normally seen to be a kind of privilege or vocation to work on Spitfires, there are very many frustrating elements which have to be dealt with if the company is to operate successfully at a commercial level – which is the actual harsh reality faced every week.

I firmly believe that none of us will become 'rich' working on Spitfires, but as long as we can remain financially viable, and continue in the vein of the past few years, then the challenge and ultimate satisfaction of what we do will have to suffice!

The hope for the coming years has to be that customers, past, present and most importantly the future ones continue to invest in their passion. It must always be remembered that no one actually *needs* a Spitfire, and that no one has one restored as a commercial exercise. The owners undertake to rebuild because they *want* to, and that, thankfully, gives us the reason to be here!

Of course, circumstances change, and Spitfires are sold periodically – there is always a ready market. But if this were not the case (bearing in mind the substantial increase in values over the past few years) then Spitfires would not be restored, and as a consequence, the restoration industry would hardly exist.

In conclusion, Airframe Assemblies would wish to acknowledge all our customers over the years who have invested in a Spitfire, and by default, in us. A mention has to go to the staff and team at AA, where skill and experience are the backbone of what we do. At the time of writing, the order book is healthy, and several other projects/rebuilds are currently under discussion. The immediate future therefore does look very positive, which we all hope will continue!

Wings

There are numerous cottage industries that support the restoration of a Spitfire. VMI Engineering is one such company, based in Hampshire, that are able to restore Spitfire fuselage and wings. Information from Ian Ward of VMI gives us a brief insight into his company and what it takes to overhaul a set of wings.

VMI Engineering was incorporated in October 2006 as a company to assist the activities of Ian Ward within the aviation industry, following his career working for the late Alan Mann. The name VMI, the initials of Ian, his partner Vicky and his only son at the time, Marcus, was given to the company. After a short spell back in general aviation at Fairoaks Airport, Chobham, an opportunity arose to assist Classic Aero Engineering at Thruxton airfield in restoring a Spitfire T9, a job kindly sought by John Williamson, a Second World War aircraft quality inspector and E4 signatory for vintage aeroplanes. Upon a steep learning curve the Spitfire was inducted into Ian's skill set in sheet metal work where a solid 10 months of commuting 100 miles a day assisted Ian in making the decision that the vintage aircraft and Spitfire world was where he would like to work his trade.

During the period at Thruxton, and meeting seasoned Spitfire restorers and owners, Ian decided to open a small industrial unit in Hampshire and obtain some sheet metal equipment. The business grew over a couple of years when the chance came to rebuild a pair of wings indirectly for the BBMF. Ian constructed them using original drawings and a pair of wing jigs using heavy box section steel where the wings could be restored. Upon completion of this task of work, and the satisfactory fitting of the wings on the newly in-house restored fuselage for the aircraft by the BBMF engineers, VMI now finds itself with a strong, skilled workforce of expertise, as well as the necessary premises and approvals awarded by the CAA to apply the skills to the ever-encompassing world of restoring vintage aeroplanes and, at the forefront of those, the Spitfire.

Restoring a wing – step-by-step

Firstly the wing has to be stripped down of all parts into each component part. This involves drilling out all the rivets and removing nuts and bolts, keeping the items tagged to assist in the reassembly at a later date. All parts are then inspected against original drawings, where available, for conformity to the original design specification.

BELOW Main spars situated in the jig. *(VMI Engineering)*

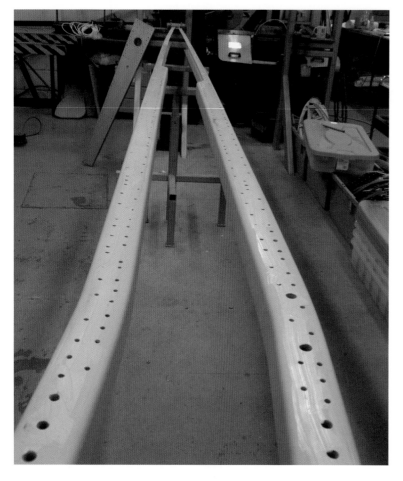

Each Spitfire component carries a part number, typically in the style as follows: 30008–579. The first three digits of the five-digit part code is designated by Spitfire type; for example, Type 300 was a very early mark of Spitfire, Type 390 a late Mark XIX Spitfire. Following this the items could be identified where they were fitted to the aircraft by the last two digits of the five-digit part code, 08 being the wings, 27 the fuselage and so on. Finally the last figures represented the drawing number.

In an ideal world each part code should correspond with the type of Spitfire wing being restored. The problems start coming when parts numbers of other previous marks of Spitfire appear on the components for any said Spitfire. The Spitfire was a constantly developing aircraft where certain areas of it were improved and modified, for instance to suit the changing armaments and power plants being fitted. Not every section of the Spitfire needed changing, though, so any parts within the wing and/or the entire aircraft that were satisfactory for purpose were left alone. This meant a lot of different-type Spitfire parts were used as the development of the airframe continued.

Where restoration can be tricky is when a late production aircraft, c1944, arrives for refurbishment – as many as 20 different variants of Spitfire parts may have been used to produce the component assemblies. Spitfire wings seem to carry the most changes of design through the aircraft development.

Once all the parts have been correctly identified then the restoration of them can begin. Following inspection, each item has to be checked for integrity, either by visual inspection, non-destructive testing, or by other means of examination. The treatments to preserve the parts are applied, along with a coat of epoxy prime. Once a sizeable kit of components is available, then the wing assembly process can really get going. Invariably, as there are many hours involved in a wing overhaul, the main spar booms, upper and lower, are replaced. This not only gives the wing a major new part of primary structure, the main wing to fuselage attachment holes can be reamed on assembly to the fuselage on the lowest nominal pin size. The wings and fuselage can be reamed up to eight times, increasing 0.004in at a time to ensure tightness of the wing pin. Once the holes are oversize the main spars would need replacing.

The main spar booms are match drilled to the old spars, taking care not to allow the relationship to differ from the original, and all the holes are pilot drilled. Each spar boom is pilot drilled and placed within the wing jig for alignment. The spar joining webs are then positioned and drilled to the spars to effect a spar boom and web assembly. All parts are then reamed together and assembled using bolts and rivets, matched from the disassembly process. Once the solid platform is in place the newly assembled and restored nose ribs are attached to the spar assembly to form the structure known as the D box. Cannon castings are installed, along with the electrical conduit tube for the navigation light wiring.

Once all the ribs are in place the D box skinning can start. The D box skins are made up from 14 SWG alloy skin seam joined at the very front of the wing with butt straps; each

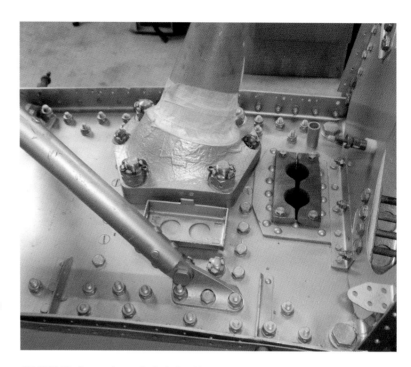

ABOVE Undercarriage pintle bolted in place. *(VMI Engineering)*

BELOW Leading edge nose ribs in position. *(VMI Engineering)*

skin is expertly shaped using an English Wheel. Only a few access holes are available for the riveting up, which can prove quite awkward for the rivet bucker.

The next stage is to position the mid-section wing ribs. Rib 1, most inboard, and ribs 14 and 19 (Aileron) are located first to ensure correct alignment for attaching the wing at the rear spar pick-up and for fitting the aileron; the rear spars are then fitted to create the 'picture frame' of structure. Once these points are set, all the other main ribs can be installed between the D box and rear spar. Most ribs are bolted in place nearer the root of the wing where rivets are preferred closer to the tip. Working from root to tip the radiator or oil cooler bays is completed, along with the wheel bay. Ammunition or long-range fuel cell bays are completed next, together with structure nearer the tip of the

ABOVE **Wing ribs being fitted.**
(VMI Engineering)

ABOVE **With all the ribs arranged you get a good idea of how many parts go into the build of a Spitfire wing.** *(VMI Engineering)*

wing. At this time the wing has some of its strength and it can be manoeuvred within the jig to the horizontal position for ease of work for the next stage.

With the wing suitably supported, the trailing edge rib area, where the flaps retract, can be installed, ensuring that the flap will close flush.

Correct alignment with the aileron must be achieved on the outer section of trailing edge. Once all the structure is secure, the wing can be repositioned vertical in the jig and all the locating points reattached prior to the skinning process. Starting at the tip, working top to bottom for access, each skin panel is drilled,

BELOW **The wing with all its ribs fitted.**
(VMI Engineering)

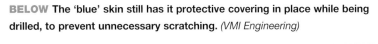

BELOW **The 'blue' skin still has it protective covering in place while being drilled, to prevent unnecessary scratching.** *(VMI Engineering)*

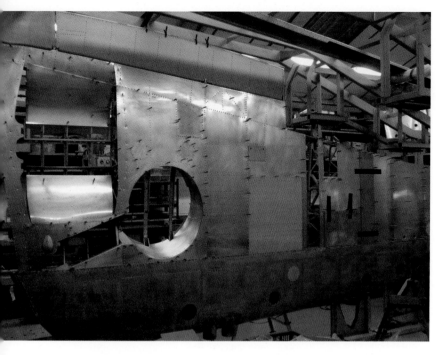

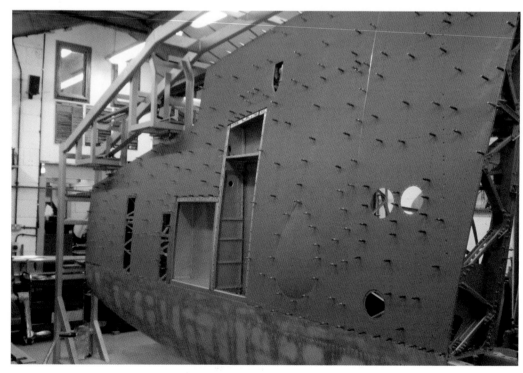

ABOVE Underside skins gripped and drilled. Wheel well and radiator shrouds are also in place. *(VMI Engineering)*

ABOVE RIGHT The original skins are gripped back in place to make sure the ribs are fitted correctly. *(VMI Engineering)*

cut and dimpled where necessary prior to fitting. Each skin is installed in the same manner making certain there is sufficient access for the rivet bucker to work. Once all the skins are put in place a trial fit of the radiator fairing for a starboard wing and oil cooler fairing on the earlier marks of Spitfire on the port wing is next. All the machine-gun access doors are tested and the quick-release fasteners are shimmed

on their latch plates to ensure necessary grip. This applies to the ammunition bay and all other access panels.

The undercarriage leg is installed and shimmed for correct operation, then the gear door can be fitted – often trimmed to suit if a new skin has been positioned on the door. Finally, all system parts are put together and checked for correct operation, flying control

RIGHT Topside of the wing with the skins held in place. *(VMI Engineering)*

cable runs are inspected for rubbing, and fairleads installed where necessary. The wing is now ready for fitting.

Having worked on the Spitfire structure for a few years now, you have to respect the designers for creating what is a complicated wing structure with no modern computer-aided software, and bringing the wing into a production environment where skilled or semi-

ABOVE LEFT Wheel well structure with the curved access panels removed. *(VMI Engineering)*

ABOVE The skins are drilled, then removed, painted and fitted. *(VMI Engineering)*

LEFT The wing nears completion and the flaps and aileron are fitted in place for clearance checks. *(VMI Engineering)*

RIGHT The aileron bell crank assembled into the wing. (VMI Engineering)

FAR RIGHT TOP Inside the wing the brown paxolin cradle supports an air bottle that supplies the aircraft's pneumatic system. (VMI Engineering)

FAR RIGHT BOTTOM Wing internal detail; the wing uses a lot of nuts and bolts in its construction. (VMI Engineering)

skilled personnel were able to mass produce the aircraft.

Each part has its own story to tell and is identified with the inspection stamp of who made or assembled it. If only the facilities and tooling was available today for the Spitfire, how much easier the work would be. Having said that, one wouldn't have the fun of working it all out!

LEFT Inside the mainplane D box looking at the nose ribs. (VMI Engineering)

BELOW Internal structure around the radiator area. (VMI Engineering)

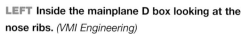

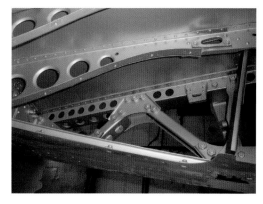

FAR LEFT More radiator housing detail: the large rib is rib 1, which is at the inboard end of the wing. *(VMI Engineering)*

LEFT Another look at rib 1 shows it is constructed with many parts bolted together. *(VMI Engineering)*

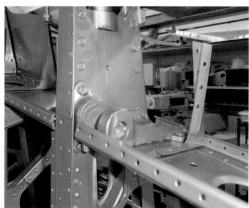

LEFT Detail around the inboard aileron hinge. *(VMI Engineering)*

LEFT Underside of the wing; the skins are gripped in place with the riveting partially completed. *(VMI Engineering)*

Re-covering flying controls with fabric

The elevator and the rudder are, again, assembled in a similar way to the ailerons, except that when the framework is pieced together, instead of being skinned with metal they are covered in fabric (although some marks of Spitfire that had rear fuselage tanks fitted had metal-skinned elevators).

Re-covering the flying controls is a job for a specialist; the fabric used is F1 Irish linen, which is expensive, so you need to make sure that you cut your fabric carefully. It is initially cut to shape, and then laid on to the flying control surface (rudder or elevator). The trailing edges are then hand sewn into place and the fabric left to settle before being shrunk with distilled water. After 24 hours the first coat of red nitrate dope is applied to the fabric. This causes the fabric to shrink further and become taut.

The next stage is to carry out rib stitching, which secures the fabric to the ribs of the

flying control. The stitching prevents the fabric 'ballooning' in flight and also stops the spread of tear damage.

After the above steps have been carried out it is time to apply the surface tapes, drain eyelets and inspection frames. The surface tapes cover and seal the fabric at the trailing edges and cover the rib stitching and anything else protruding above the structure. They provide extra strength and also stop the risk of the base fabric chafing through.

Drain eyelets are fitted at the trailing edges of the controls, on the underside, to enable drainage to occur. Inspection frames (if required) allow the fitment of a fabric patch, which can be removed to allow the inspection of the inside of the flying control without damaging the base fabric.

Once these processes have been carried out, several more coats of dope are applied. Each coat is sanded down in between, to bring the finish up to the desired result.

Finally, two coats of silver dope are administered to help to protect against ultra-

BELOW TE311's fuselage waiting for frame 5 (the engine bulkhead) to be fitted. *(Paul Blackah)*

violet (UV) damage. The flying control is now complete and ready for painting.

Chief Technician and co-author Paul Blackah has been working with historic aircraft since 1982, specialising in the airframe itself, and gives here a short insight into working on the Spitfire's airframe:

I began working with the Spitfire airframe in 1993, when I first joined the RAF BBMF. The day-to-day work carried out on the airframe itself varies greatly from actually working on an airframe that is stripped for restoration.

On a day-to-day basis, when working on the airframe, it's a case of looking for loose rivets, replacing them, ensuring that there are no cracks in the skin or structure that need addressing either by repair or replacing etc; basically just everyday care and maintenance. At no point does the airframe require stripping down at BBMF; this would only happen when an aircraft is on a major servicing with an outside company.

The aim is to maintain the aircraft from one major servicing to another without, where possible, any significant work being carried out. Working on TE311 was therefore a huge learning curve for me, albeit a very useful and constructive one.

I now have a better understanding of how the Spitfire is constructed and the quirks and foibles that the aircraft presents. This, in turn, has helped in working with the other aircraft on the Flight. The knowledge I have gained has helped fine tune other aircraft's airframes within the flight.

One of the most important lessons that I have learnt, and passed on to others, is that the restorer MUST make use of the available drawings in conjunction with the manuals, as there is so much useful information in there, which makes the task easier.

Although the restoration of TE311 has taken 11 years, the knowledge and experience gained has more than made up for the time spent on the project.

BELOW TE311 fuselage from the left; behind the fuselage are the remaining skins waiting to be put in. *(Paul Blackah)*

Chapter Six

Aircraft components

In this chapter we will give you a brief insight into what processes go into the restoring of some of the aircraft's internal components. It would be impossible to touch on every individual item needing attention during a restoration project. However, the main principle applies to all, whether it be a small special washer or a large complex machined part; each will require the same care and attention to achieve the finished result.

OPPOSITE Arthur Allabedyev of Supermarine Aero Engineering machines parts for a Spitfire spinner assembly. *(Supermarine Aero Engineering)*

RIGHT Pilot's seat being riveted by Ron Wallis. Note, this seat is metal in construction instead of the composite 'aero plastic' seats. *(Airframe Assemblies)*

Overhauling/manufacturing internal systems

BELOW The seat is handmade. Michael Jacobs is dressing one of the pans. *(Airframe Assemblies)*

BELOW RIGHT Michael Jacobs of Airframe Assemblies dressing the seat pan. *(Airframe Assemblies)*

Supermarine Aero Engineering Ltd is a company that produces the majority of components for the Spitfire restorer, whether working to drawings or from patterns taken from original parts. Mark Harris, owner of the company, tells us how his interest in the Spitfire began, why he set the company up, and a little about the process involved in manufacturing new parts for the Spitfire:

My own involvement with the Spitfire began when I found myself agreeing to build one for a local businessman and friend, the late Peter Sadler. I had recently completed for him an American kit helicopter and couldn't at the time think of anything more interesting to do!

At 16 years old I began an Engineering Apprenticeship with GEC where I was fortunate enough to be trained and qualified as both a Toolmaker and a Development Engineer. Through college I attained a HNC in mechanical engineering design, although my eventual job at the firm was to be a Production Engineer; this entailed turning designs into finished products, made in a huge variety of ways on both large and small production lines.

I became redundant at the age of 24 and then founded my own engineering company. Over the next eight very hard years I undertook a huge range of projects from high-volume component manufacture, fabrication and race car engineering. I gained a University degree, but by 1996 my eye had been turned and my

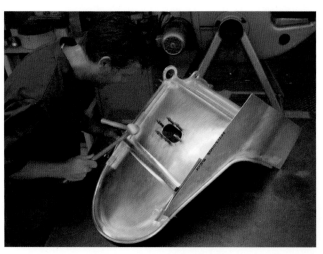

RIGHT Undercarriage locking mechanism body, again created from a forging like the pintle assembly, to give the part strength. *(Supermarine Aero Engineering)*

passion for engineering was focused on nothing but the Spitfire.

Peter had purchased the stock, work in progress, tooling and drawings off a company that had over several years rebuilt a number of Spitfires. He had also managed to secure the name Supermarine. We now had in our possession more Spitfire parts than I cared to count; most were of original wartime manufacture, but their grand total was well short of what would be needed to build a complete aircraft. In addition to the original parts we purchased, were a large number of 'new made parts'; these were supported by very well produced engineering drawings and carried all the correct paperwork. I would later learn that despite their promising appearance they were typical of most of what had been made after the war by various companies and individuals. In basic design, parts like these match original detail, but are different enough not to be interchangeable. For a new-build aircraft these parts can be 'worked in' by bastardising their mating parts, with the effect of changing a whole assembly. This for a one-off and unique solution may not have been of any serious consideration to the aircraft's rebuilders, whose brief was to return the aircraft to a safe flying condition. However, despite looking every inch the wonderfully iconic fighter we all know and love, its thousands of working parts and mechanisms could be best described as 'in the spirit of original' rather than being in any way the same as the original. Spitfires are well-engineered machines, but were not built to be maintenance free; the RAF therefore provided its stores with a generous supply of every part most likely to wear out or be damaged on a regular basis.

The interchangeability of parts has been at the very core of successful production engineering for over 200 years; it allowed the Industrial Revolution, and certainly enabled aircraft like the Spitfire, to have its components made in obscure locations all over the country and be assembled on production lines by

LEFT AND ABOVE
This is how many components need to be made to produce an instrument panel anti-vibration mount. *(Supermarine Aero Engineering)*

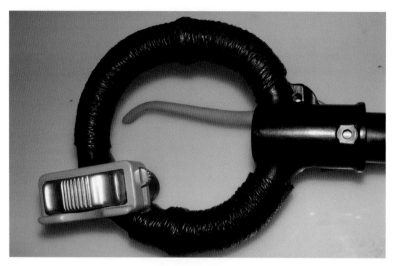

ABOVE Not original,
but new, manufactured
spade grip, complete
with firing button
and brake lever.
*(Supermarine Aero
Engineering)*

ABOVE RIGHT
Rudder control tube
guides. Note, even
new items have their
part number etched on
them, plus the identity
of the company
that manufactured
them. In this case
S.A.E., Supermarine
Aero Engineering.
*(Supermarine Aero
Engineering)*

largely inexperienced workers very quickly.
As the complexities of what Peter and I had
undertaken began to become clear we both
decided that the only way forward was,
wherever possible, the absolute adherence to
that same component principle.

Supermarine Aero Engineering's early life
was, in hindsight, a kind of honeymoon. Peter
and I had, by necessity, to learn very quickly
about both the Spitfire and the rapidly developing
restoration industry that was probably looking at
our efforts to collect original drawings, parts and
data with a degree of suspicion. While Peter's
interest in Supermarine was predominantly
getting his own Spitfire, we had both become
preoccupied with the idea of a spares business,
putting back into production replacement parts
that not only looked exactly the same as originals,
but more importantly had the same mechanical
and dimensional specifications.

Unexpectedly Peter was forced to retire from

Supermarine Aero Engineering Ltd in March
2000 and I bought from him sole control of
the business and assets. Using my knowledge
of production engineering and continuing
the work Peter and I had started I began to
make and stock original specification standard
parts, most needed by owners and restorers
around the world. Over the previous four years
Supermarine had obtained both an ISO and
Civil Aviation Authority approval and was, under
UK Air Law, one of the very few companies able
to make, stock and supply parts to operators
and restorers of aircraft like the Spitfire.

In Britain at this time there exists an ever
growing population of people who have
forgotten their primeval instinct for creativity.
To compound this problem the Spitfire and its
component parts were made by a generation
of highly skilled men and women working within
an unbroken framework of training dating back
to the birth of Britain's Industrial Revolution.
These were skills passed on from father to son,
master to apprentice, in a Britain that still led
the world, not only with its huge Empire but by
its superlative manufacturing might.

As I began to build my new business I
needed to overcome three basic problems, the
first of which was financial; buying Supermarine
had pretty much used up every penny I had
and engineering is expensive.

Secondly, I needed customers, ones
requiring an 'off the shelf' service, or the

LEFT Newly manufactured filtered assembly.
(Supermarine Aero Engineering)

'standard parts', that I made to order. Unfortunately at that time most owners and operators had no confidence in a new company being able to produce parts 'off the shelf' rather than the 'made to measure' methods they had always used. I needed to convince a sceptical industry on the advantages of 'standardisation'.

Thirdly, as the orders began to come in I needed skilled engineers. As difficult as the first two problems proved, finding good engineers would be not only my greatest challenge, but would seriously restrict my company's growth.

At the time of writing this piece Supermarine is 16 years old. During that time I have advertised, interviewed, work trialled, employed and lost more people than I care to remember; skill shortages affect virtually every engineering company in Britain, particularly so for specialists like historic aviation businesses.

Today I have ten full-time and several part-time staff; very few engineers nowadays, even the most skilled, have got the depth of knowledge needed to properly manufacture parts for the Spitfire. For not only does the work needed cover a vast spectrum of disciplines, but those disciplines have all too often not been practised for over 60 years. Eventually of course the right people do come along and join our highly skilled team. Apprentices normally start after college and learn their skills as they would have done 70 years ago. However, as young engineers in a small factory producing potentially every part for the Spitfire, the range of skills I expect them to master is probably far greater than would have been required at one of the big aircraft factories in the 1930s and '40s.

So what makes a typical day at Supermarine? With customers all over the world we try to offer as long a working day as is reasonably possible; the workshop is open from 8am to about 8pm, Monday to Friday. But, thanks to the internet, and Andrew Nicklin's tireless efforts, ringing, emailing or faxing during office hours and he's normally able to answer anything Spitfire. As Supermarine's General Manager, he has used other members of staff plus his vast 'techie brain' to construct the biggest Spitfire databases known to man since the 1940s. I have known Andy since we both built Minis in the 1980s; he came to help sort me out in 2005 and will probably retire doing so. I think it's fair to say that while I started Supermarine off in its current direction it has been Andy who has turned the company into a functioning commercial business.

Design and Development is an ongoing and all-encompassing role. I have the dubious title of both Chief Executive and Design and Development Manager. The Chief Executive title is far too grand for a little factory like mine. Design and Development: the design title does not really apply here as nobody needs to redesign the Spitfire, the original seems to have done a pretty good job over the years. What we can do is collect and record original data and so reconstruct the vast archive of original data lost and destroyed after the war once the need for a piston engine aircraft, like the Spitfire, had declined.

The job of Design and Development Manager is actually one of recapturing original designs and developing ways of remanufacturing those designs. The trick is to do so cost effectively,

ABOVE LEFT AND ABOVE The wooden/metal mould to enable the manufacture of spinner shells.
(Paul Blackah)

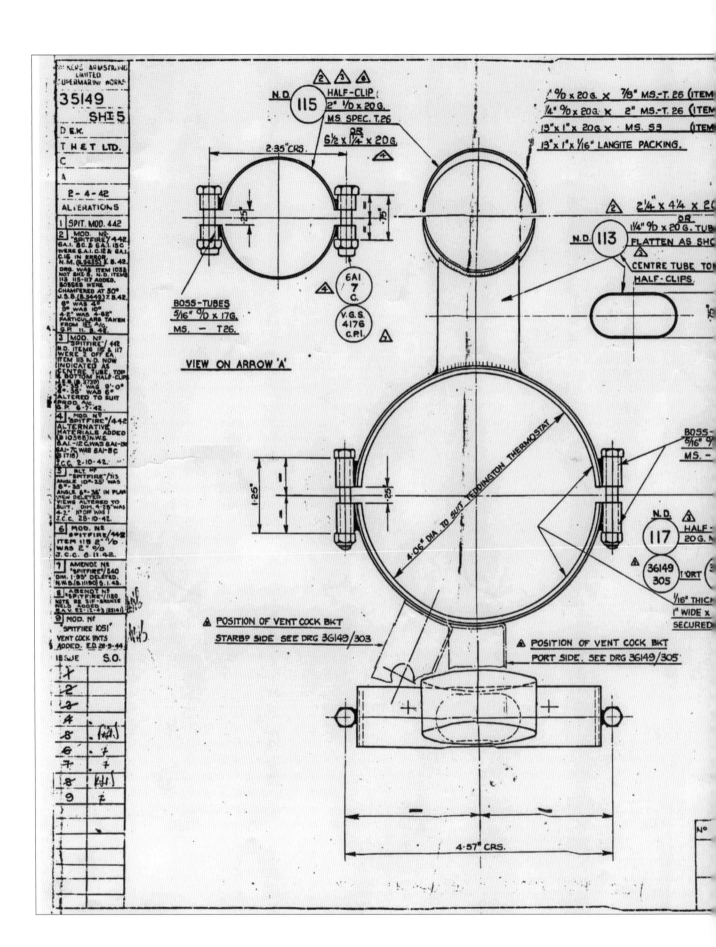

VIEW ON ARROW 'A'

POSITION OF VENT COCK BKT
STARBD SIDE SEE DRG 36149/303

POSITION OF VENT COCK BKT
PORT SIDE. SEE DRG 36149/305

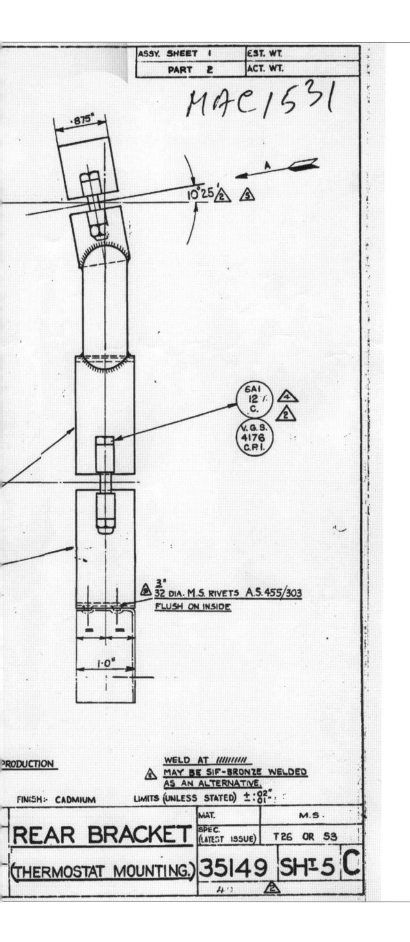

at the same time trying to match or exceed original specifications. The other vital feature of what we all must do in this industry is maintain the exact look of these wonderfully iconic aeroplanes and the parts that comprise them.

When the first batch of Spitfires were ordered Vickers Supermarine gave them the type number 300; this prefixing system enabled the factory to control the allocation of parts, it was a method that had worked well for many years and would continue throughout the war years and beyond. As new types came along each would be given a new number (the Mark IX, for example, was 361). The factory also had a secondary system in place to show a part's general position on the aircraft – 08 for instance, relates to the bottom outer mainplane, while 12 relates to the bottom outer aileron. The numbers were used by Vickers Supermarine for other earlier aeroplanes; for example, 11 was used for top outer ailerons. More observant readers will probably have noticed that there is no top outer aileron on a low-wing monoplane and so this number would never be used for the Spitfire. Next was the need for a part number that was simpler; draughtsmen simply took the next number off a list. Generally speaking the use of even numbers went to port with odd numbers going to starboard. So if we see a pin assembly with the number of 30012-129 we know it relates to a Mark I Spitfire (300), aileron, (12) and part (129, starboard). It is actually the outboard hinge pin assembly, a part that remained unchanged as the Mark II was introduced. It was considered suitable for all marks and can be found on every Spitfire from Mark I to PR Mark XIX.

Fortunately, the RAF Museum at Hendon saved from destruction many thousands of original wartime drawings. These drawings are not necessarily of the latest issue and no original data has survived that controls the Spitfire's true design state, but thanks to their endeavours we are able to use this incredible archive as a base for all the missing information.

LEFT Component drawings are essential, especially if the items are missing or badly damaged.

Obviously we always start any remanufacturing process by looking through the Hendon archive. Some proprietary parts suppliers such as Dunlop made many parts for the Spitfire, occasionally these investigations lead to a positive result; however, all too often we cannot find any original drawing and so begins the process of redrawing the part from original pattern parts.

When looking at original parts that are in good condition they can be considered as frozen moments in time, if such parts are then considered with a good working knowledge of their function, together with all mating parts; one can, thanks to the limits and fits prescribed by Vickers Supermarine together with a good working knowledge of the aircraft, be pretty confident that new engineering drawings will produce parts virtually identical to the originals. Over the years we have done this many times. We currently list about 8,000 parts in our standard product range, that is to say parts that have been examined, drawn and made, including special tools, fixtures and inspection gauges. After a new batch of parts has cleared inspection they are added to our stock list; this will hopefully ensure we can keep up with any future demand. Finally, we collect up all of that tooling and the original parts that made it all

These three pictures show that to fabricate a small clamp you still have to produce a jig to get the correct angles required for assembly. (*Supermarine Aero Engineering*)

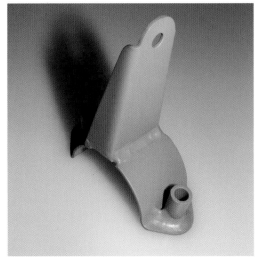

possible, add the original parts that have their own database and stores for future reference.

The role of Production Manager goes to another Andy, this time Andrew Minton; he joined the company in 2000 and, with the exception of myself, knows more about what makes Supermarine tick than anyone. The job of Production Manager here is very complex; not only is it necessary for him to plan and produce job cards for each component required, he takes care of the procurement of materials, looks after all of the company's subcontracts and controls the Bonded Materials Store. This is very useful when overseeing production in that he is able to take a holistic view of the production process. As jobs unfold and specialist tooling is produced it becomes necessary to buy or manufacture this tooling; this is recorded, photographed and numbered in such a way as to enable its reuse the next time a particular part or assembly is made.

In order to provide a better insight into how we organise our business I have produced a very brief breakdown of the infrastructure required to manufacture parts for the Spitfire, which is as follows:

Demand from customers or our own instinct as to what will be needed next, starts the process of remanufacture. Andy Nicklin will often ask existing owners, operators and restorers to gauge their needs, but more often than not we are led by our customer's requests. Obviously the potential parts usage for the Spitfire industry is huge; with 17,000 part numbers per plane over the many different marks in use all over the world, the range of daily requests can be many and varied. However, it is neither practical nor commercially possible to make everything. Lots of proprietary parts still exist; and specialist companies are around to deal with parts such as engine, propeller, radiator, tank, wings, fuselage and tailplane.

A typical need for our services would be either where it is more cost effective to have us manufacture one of our standard parts and so avoid the burdensome work of special permissions to remanufacture, produce drawings, do material investigations, produce any specialist tooling and have to overproduce to justify set-up costs. Or when a part is already available off the shelf we can provide a

ABOVE AND LEFT
Hydraulic pump union under manufacture and the amount of detail that goes into the finished item.
(Supermarine Aero Engineering)

same day dispatch with release paperwork to anywhere in the world.

The parts we try to keep in stock, or plan to produce next, are ones most requested by customers; we always try to keep up, but naturally demand often outstrips supply and delivery may take a few weeks when a more common part goes out of stock. More unusual items may take considerably longer, particularly so when, for example, we are supplying something like a full aircraft pipe and bracket set comprising hundreds of complex handmade pieces. Forward-thinking owners and restorers always work in conjunction with suppliers' lead times, especially when the parts they need are so difficult to find, but inevitably there are always a few last minute rush jobs before an aircraft's first flight. As for the remaining thousands of parts not yet manufactured, we are doing our very best. However, the task is huge. I don't expect to ever complete the task and can only apologise for not yet holding some obscure variant of a seldom-used bracket in stock; for everything else we are working our way through.

New enquiry leading to new manufacture

Whenever an order is processed we enter its details on a Contract Review form; this captures all pertinent information, quantity, delivery, price, special shipping details etc. However, for parts not yet on the company's radar we must begin a line of investigation prior to any work; this also follows a contract review process and would typically comprise the following steps:

■ Do we know the part's original and correct part number?
■ Is the part listed in any original manuals, drawings, modification notes or mandatory controls?
■ What material is used? If none is listed or if that material is obsolete, a suitable replacement must be found. This could be determined by either evaluation of the stresses involved, so as to calculate a suitable replacement, or by material analysis at an independent laboratory, or using a combination of the two.
■ What was the original method of

manufacture and why was that method used? Cast, forged, fabricated or machined, choices were made for a variety of reasons, sometimes for strength, sometimes for efficiency given the volumes and options available. Today, volumes are lower but no compromise on strength or performance can be considered.
■ Where no drawing exists one must be produced.
■ Is the material available from our on-site Bonded Material Stores? (A locked and controlled material stores; every part manufactured for use on a flying aircraft must, by Air Law, be traceable back to its place of origin and be supported by a chemical analysis.) If more stock is to be purchased, from where and at what cost?
■ Tooling can often be discounted; for example, in the case of thread cutting, no special purchase is required where a part may need a very common form. However, in the case of a fuselage, the tooling, timescales, supporting data and infrastructure required by far outweighs the finished job.
■ Production of new parts not previously manufactured by our company can, where those parts are complex, take many months, not necessarily because of excessive man hours, but due to the development element of such work. It is often incredibly frustrating to see a job go through many cycles of stopping and starting while new tooling is ordered, materials are sent off for secondary plating work, or more vital information about some critical detail is sought, often only to reveal that previously gathered information is either incorrect or not able to solve the problem. Such is the nature of development work; at times one's mind is haunted by the unfathomable solution, but eventually a solution comes and the job continues, although by then it's been replaced by several others.
■ Development once complete is documented and all available information is passed over to Production; small concessions often arise as first-off bugs are refined, but this phase of the work should begin to yield the benefits of everything invested into the job thus far.

- Upon completion of manufacture the complete job together with all its supporting paperwork is submitted to our Inspection Department. Every detail is checked against the drawing: dimensional, material specification, pressure testing, X-ray or magnetic particle etc. No part will ever leave the premises without passing its inspection.
- Most parts require some form of surface treatment: cadmium plating, anodising, paintwork etc; this work is done where practical prior to dispatch or entry into our Bonded Component Stores (parts ready to be fitted, subject to local conditions, to a flying aircraft).
- Only when all of the above has been complete will a part or assembly be added to the 8,000 parts listed on our production database.

I started this business, if indeed it can be called a business, without the funding or infrastructure probably needed. It has been a real struggle, not only for me but for many here, past and present, that have shared my belief in what is possible. My Dad, Peter, has worked alongside me since retiring 12 years ago from his own business; since then he has amazed all, doing everything from building work to fuselage construction. This business has enabled me to play a very small part in an incredible story; the work has allowed me to touch history and to keep it alive. I've been honoured to meet a few of the men and women who made it all happen and have the good fortune to work alongside current engineers whose skill and dedication will preserve history for future generations.

Radiators and oil coolers

These items are probably the hardest items to source, because radiators held a water coolant mix that when drained left water inside, which led to corrosion. A lot of Spitfires at the end of their 'life', to stop them from flying

BELOW Coolant radiator (large) bolted to the smaller oil cooler, as fitted to the Mark IX. *(Paul Blackah)*

RIGHT Undercarriage pintle in place; the undercarriage leg is fitted to the pintle and rotates on it. *(Paul Blackah)*

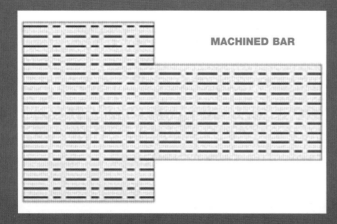

FORGED BAR

MACHINED BAR

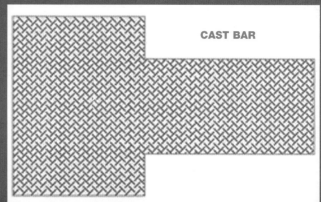

CAST BAR

MANUFACTURING AN UNDERCARRIAGE PINTLE FROM A FORGING

A forged bar gives you compressed grain flow and increased strength (see figure 1, Forged bar), whereas a machined bar renders the material more liable to fatigue and stress corrosion cracking (see figure 2, A machined bar). A cast bar has no grain flow or directional strength, so this would be no good for making an undercarriage pintle (see figure 3, A cast bar).

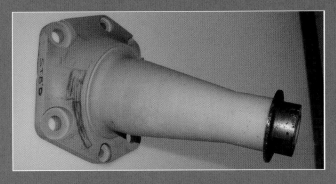

Prototype

This shows a nylon prototype, in which the manufacturing procedure is proved before starting work on the real forging.

The Forging

This shows Brookes Forgings of Halesowen, West Midlands, striking a bare forging. The strikes are aimed to replicate the original grain structure of the original component. Extra test pieces are also struck at the same time so that tensile tests can be carried out to ensure that the forging meets the required specification.

Forging after clean-up

This forging is designed as a generic base for all pintles used on all marks of Spitfires.

Tooling fixture

This shows a tooling fixture being used in one of the lathes to produce the basic outline shape and bearing surfaces; again, in every case, all fixtures and tooling have to be created to cope with all variations of the component across the complete range of Spitfire variants.

Nearing completion

This shows the turned, final bearing surface, fillet radius and oleo mounting nut thread machined.

Lathe work complete

The pintle after the completion of the lathe work. Here you can see the completed form of the conical section, the nut thread and the internal profile.

Milling

The pintle is then moved on to the milling machine and another fixture is required to machine the mounting holes and recesses. Again, the fixture is designed to allow all pintle types to be created.

Finished item

After cadmium plating (to DEF-STAN 03-19) non-destructive testing is carried out to inspect for cracks and flaws, followed by a full QA procedure, which checks that all the pintle's dimensions are within the laid-down tolerances of the drawing. The pintle is then ready for supplying to the customer with full release documentation, which is known as the CoC: Certificate of Conformity.

Photos: Supermarine Aero Engineering

again, had their radiators deliberately damaged with a pickaxe.

If you are lucky enough to have an original radiator, without damage, the item should be pressure tested, which is done by filling the radiator, blanking off all the ports and fitting one of the connections with an adaptor so that you can connect it to a foot pump. The radiator is then pressure tested by pumping air into it to 30psi and, hopefully, it won't leak! The same

test is carried out on the intercooler radiator, if one is fitted, and the oil cooler.

If, however, your radiator/oil cooler leaks it will then need repairing by a specialist company. If it is damaged beyond repair then you will need to get a new one manufactured. At the time of writing this book, the main source of newly manufactured oil coolers and radiators and also repairs of the same is a company called Anglia Radiators based in Cambridge.

RIGHT **Pair of oil coolers fixed to the Mark IIa.** *(Paul Blackah)*

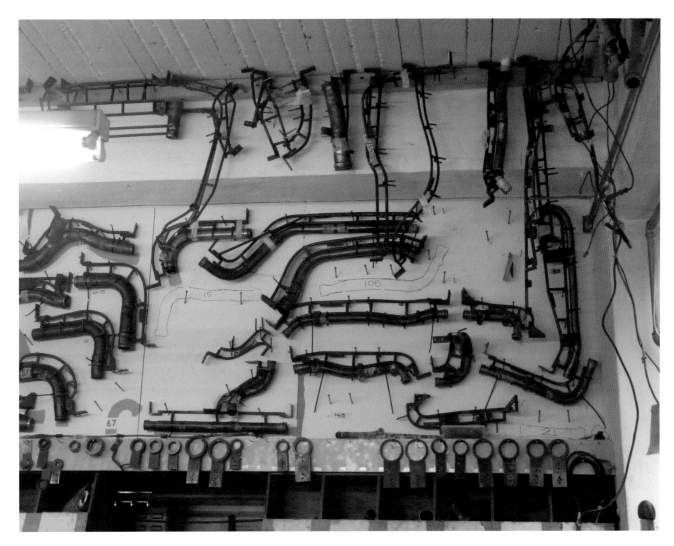

Manufacturing pipes

Most of the pipes on the Spitfire, for the hydraulic, oil, pneumatic and coolant systems are made from copper or tungum and can range from a diameter of ¼in to around 2in. On later Spitfires some of the copper/tungum pipes are manufactured from aluminium alloy.

The small-diameter pipes, especially if they are copper, can be made easily. Larger-diameter pipes, however, require specialist jigs to give the correct bends and routing of the pipe. To save yourself a lot of time and expense, in manufacturing the jigs in order to get the correct profile of each pipe, it is much quicker and simpler to use a specialist company such as Supermarine Aero Engineering, who have a supply of ready-made parts.

Flexible hoses for the fuel, hydraulic and pneumatic systems can be produced using

ABOVE Coolant and oil pipe jigs at Supermarine Aero Engineering. These jigs ensure the pipes are the correct shape. *(Paul Blackah)*

BELOW Coolant pipe in its manufacturing jig. *(Supermarine Aero Engineering)*

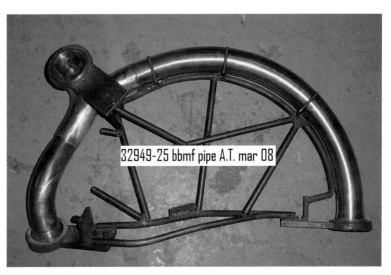

32949-25 bbmf pipe A.T. mar 08

BELOW Aeroquip
reusable pipe fitting
and 302/303 hose are
required for fuel, oil
and air pipes. *(Paul
Blackah)*

reusable end fittings. Once these pipes are manufactured they are pressure tested to one and a half times the system pressure. These hoses are replaced every six years.

Because you are using new hose and end fittings they should be submitted as a modification to the CAA. The most common hose fitted is Aeroquip 302 and 303 hose, depending on diameter, and the end fittings are EO-202 for straight fittings, EO-206 for 45° fittings and EO-208 for 90° fittings.

All the hose and fittings are available from companies like Light Aerospares (LAS) or Saywells, which keep the majority of these items in stock.

Some of the larger hose fittings may take a long time to make, so don't leave the manufacturing of pipe work too late or you may be held up in your restoration work due to the lack of one part.

Fuel tank

The majority of Spitfires have two metal fuel tanks that sit one on top of each other in front of the cockpit. Some marks of Spitfire have a different fuel capacity; for example, the bottom tank is larger on some marks, holding from 37 gallons to 48 gallons, and the top tank is smaller on some marks, because of where the oil tank fits. This is predominantly on Griffon-engined Spitfires, where the fuel capacity of the

LEFT Top fuel tank and oil tank for a Griffon-engined Spitfire. *(Supermarine Aero Engineering)*

THIS PAGE A lower 48-gallon fuel tank being constructed by welding. *(Supermarine Aero Engineering)*

top tank goes from 48 gallons to 36 gallons; however, this is compensated for by the fitment of extra tanks in the wings.

The type of fuel tanks to be fitted depends on what mark of Spitfire you have. For the purpose of this book we will describe just the top and bottom tanks. Both tanks are of metal construction and, if they have been left empty for a long time, could have a lot of corrosion. The bottom tank should have a rubberised/fabric coating applied; in order to examine the external structure this should be taken off. There are inspection panels in both tanks and on the bottom tank a fuel contents float, and there could be an electric pump. With the panels, float and pump removed it is possible to see the internal structure of the fuel tank. If the tank is corroded or badly damaged then it should, obviously, be replaced. Again,

to be rectified, which may mean applying a sealant on the inside of the tank or replacing rivets. The test is carried out again once the sealant has 'cured' and is implemented as many times as is necessary. Even new tanks can have many pressure tests, until they are ready to use.

Undercarriage – overhaul or source?

The main undercarriage legs are becoming more difficult to source and, to date, the authors are not aware of any business that produces the body casing. But *beware* – there are people who will try and sell you undercarriage legs for your project and, in seeing them only in an assembled condition, you do not know what they are like inside and it could cost you more in the long term. So if your project has undercarriage legs, once they are stripped, even if they appear to be in bad order, there are companies that can restore them back to a usable condition.

The main problems with the legs will be internal corrosion of the bore, pitting and peeling of the chrome on the sustaining ram (the fesculised portion of the leg), and wear and corrosion on the axles, especially if the wheels have been in place for many years. Least important is if the two rubber seals in the leg are perished; they can be easily replaced.

All the damage needs to be measured to see how deep it goes. This is where your air publications become useful. The AP1803N has a section on repairing the legs, which includes all the fits and tolerances allowable, plus all the repair fits and tolerances permitted, so even if your undercarriage legs look awful they may not be as bad as you think and may be repairable within the limits laid down. The sort of repairs that can be carried out are honing the bore out to a different, larger, diameter on the leg body. If this is done you will have to replace the three-part piston, to match the diameter, on the sustaining ram to the bore of the leg body. Holes for torque links, uplocks and downlocks can, if worn, be taken out to allow for the fit of oversize bolts. Chroming on the sustaining

you could build the fuel tanks yourself or go to a specialist company such as Airframe Assemblies and Arco.

The new tank(s) will come pressure tested and, in the case of the bottom tank, re-covered with the fabric and rubber coating. If the fuel tank is in good condition after investigation then the inspection panels are refitted and any other open port (such as where the float and pump fits) is sealed off and the tank is pressure tested to approximately 5psi. If the pressure holds then the tank is sound. If the pressure drops then there is a leak, which means that if air is discharging then fuel will also seep out. These leaks will have to be found by using Snoop, which is like a soapy water that bubbles when air is escaping, a similar principle to testing a bicycle tube for a puncture. Any leaks will have

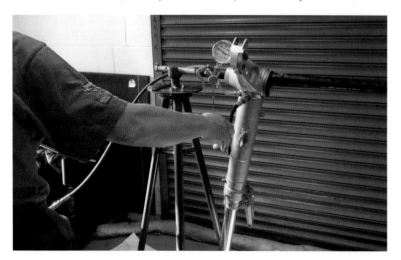

RIGHT Newly manufactured retraction jack body.
(Supermarine Aero Engineering)

ram can be replaced, as can damage to the axle bearing surfaces.

The same processes can be carried out on both a fixed strut and a retractable tail leg system as well as the main tail retraction jacks. Replacement seals, for the undercarriage system, can be obtained from companies such as Supermarine Engineering Ltd and Butser Rubber Ltd. These companies will have produced moulds from original drawings or patterns to produce these seals.

Wheels

As with undercarriage legs, the wheels are becoming harder to find and, again depending on what mark of Spitfire you have, depend on the size of main wheel that is fitted. The tail wheel is the same for all marks of Spitfire.

Wheels are prone to corrosion as they are manufactured from magnesium. The wheels should be inspected for cracking, by NDT techniques, and corrosion. Any corrosion should be removed carefully, ensuring that the

RIGHT 10¼in brake carrier being machined.
(Supermarine Aero Engineering)

BELOW Brake carrier nearing completion.
(Supermarine Aero Engineering)

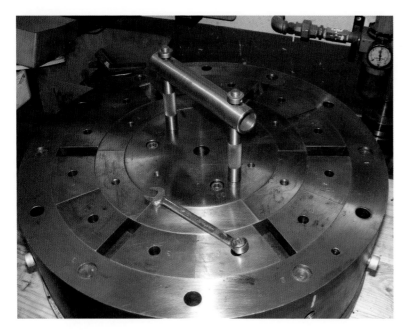

wheel remains within limits afterwards. Any small cracks that are found can be blended out, provided they are not in critical areas, for example around the rim where the tyre sits.

If your wheels are too badly damaged it is worth considering getting newly manufactured wheels from companies such as Retro Track and Air. You may also want to give thought to going tubeless on your new wheels, as inner tubes are also extremely hard to source. New tubeless wheels have been in use for over a year and are proving very satisfactory at RAF BBMF. Tyres for your Spitfire are still manufactured by Dunlop Aircraft Tyres Ltd, so there is a plentiful supply, which are available at aviation tyre suppliers such as Watts Aviation.

Perspexes – blowing new canopies

The Perspex on your Spitfire will almost certainly need replacing, due to the fact that it will have degraded and if kept in sunlight over the last 50 years will have become opaque. The making of a Perspex canopy or shaped panel should be done by a specialist company such as White Ellerton. They produce a mould of the shape required and use a process called drape forming, where the Perspex is applied as a hot sheet over the mould, which then settles into shape with the help of several layers of mould cloth.

Another technique that can be used is blow forming, where the sheet of Perspex is clamped on a table and air is blown under it until it makes the shape of the mould.

Flat windscreen panels can be made quite easily by the restorer.

LEFT **Certificates of Conformity (CoC) are required for all components manufactured for your project.**

Bearings

All the aircraft bearings will require replacement. There are a lot of bearing companies that can supply bearings and you must be aware that, as in many things, you can buy the correct part number bearing with a price that differs greatly from place to place; however, in this case there really is a difference in the quality dependent on price.

Flying control cables

The flying control cables on your project will either not be there – cut through when the aircraft was moved – or, if they are extant, will be badly corroded and will not be able to be used. Original cables were spliced, which is a way of tying off the end of cables where the cable is wrapped round an eye end and then fastened back into itself, with the tied area being wrapped in cotton thread. This technique has been superseded by swaging, which is basically crimping an end fitting on to the end of the cable. Swaged cables are easier to manufacture whereas splicing is fast becoming a dying art.

The main manufacturer for flying controls in this country is Bruntons.

Instruments and electrical equipment

Instruments should be calibrated prior to fitment to ensure that they read precisely; you don't want a fuel tank to read full when it's really half empty. The generators need to be tested so that they give out the correct electrical output. There are companies that are able to do the testing by sending them the equipment and instruments and when they are returned will provide the appropriate paperwork.

Certificate of Conformity

Why is the CoC so important? Because every part you have manufactured, no matter how large or small, needs this paperwork to prove not only traceability but also that it has been manufactured according to the correct specifications as laid down by the original drawings, or if produced from a pattern, that it is to an equivalent standard as the original. If applicable it also provides information on what testing has been carried out. This includes any NDTs or pressure tests, leak tests etc. If there is a problem with any of the components you therefore have the means to return to the company and query their processes should anything fail or not fit correctly.

Individual companies produce their own CoCs and they differ in layout, but they are basically all the same and accepted by the CAA.

BELOW With the CoC you can trace how your items are manufactured, plus they aid with the CAA audits and inspections.

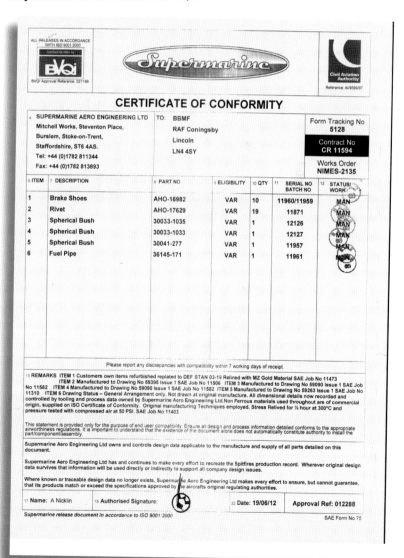

Chapter Seven

Assembly

So, your wings and fuselage are due to be completed shortly, the engine and propeller have been overhauled and all the system components are ready to be installed. There are certain items of specialist equipment that will be required to help with the assembly and the functional checks that are required afterwards. It is just as important to plan the assembly of your aircraft as it was to plan the stripping down of parts. This is where experience and advice, perhaps from someone more knowledgeable than you, can be invaluable.

OPPOSITE Cowling fastener receptacles still to be fitted, along with the cowling diaphragm. Note, there are no oil or coolant pipes in place at this stage. *(Paul Blackah)*

ABOVE **The pilot's seat complete with armour plate and starter handle fitted. The aircraft's battery is to the right of the seat.**
(Paul Blackah)

Assembly equipment

Just as you required certain specialised tools and equipment for the strip of your aircraft, you will also need certain apparatus for the rebuild. It is, in fact, more important at the rebuild to have the correct equipment available than at the strip, as it is essential that the aircraft is put together correctly and this is only achieved with the right tools.

You will need a pair of 5-tonne jacks and an adjustable tail trestle to enable you to place the aircraft in the 'rigging' position, which is in a flight position. To obtain this you will also require rigging boards and a clinometer, which help set the fuselage in both axes at the correct angle. The clinometer will also be used when checking the range of movements of the flying controls. A tensiometer will make sure the flying control cables are tensioned correctly.

Also on your list should be at least one pair of wing trestles, preferably two, to hold up the wings while they are being fitted and then to support the aircraft as it is being worked on. You will need a set of wing bolt reamers (two sets of eight of these just in case the holes need to be reamed oversize; each reamer is four thousandths of an inch bigger in diameter than the previous one) for reaming out the main spar bolt holes for when the wings are fitted.

Prop fitting tools are required: a special spanner and torque wrench. A foot pump is essential to pressurise the coolant system and a hydraulic rig to carry out hydraulic tests on the system. An air charging rig is needed to fill the pneumatic system. Lastly, a decent tool kit with the full range of spanners, sockets etc.

Now, finally, it is time to put it all together.

Fitting out the aircraft

The following is not necessarily the order that everyone would assemble an aircraft in, but as a rough guide it gives an idea of the process.

RIGHT **This original radio unit could be fitted, but not used.**
(Paul Blackah)

LEFT **Wiring looms
being installed on
TE311.** *(Paul Blackah)*

Your fuselage and wings will arrive from the
restorer on the back of a lorry and a crane or
a forklift will be needed to transfer the 'shell' of
your aircraft to your workshop, where it will be
placed on its two jacks and tail trestle. From
there you can commence to install the systems
into the fuselage.

A good place to start is with the electrical
system, which, because the fuselage is bare,
makes fitting the wiring looms and all its
terminal boxes straightforward; you are able to
route the cabling and clip it in where required
with ease.

Depending on whether your project has a

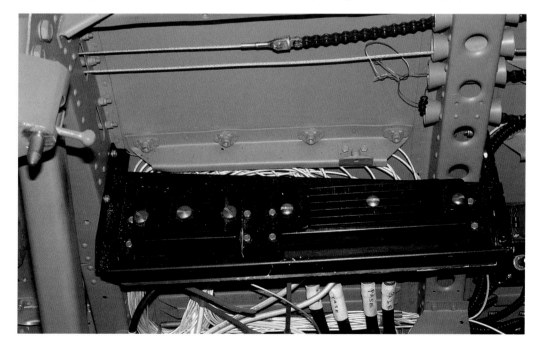

LEFT **Wiring to the
main fuse box.** *(Paul
Blackah)*

ABOVE Back of the instrument panel with all the wiring and pipework connected. The disconnected pipe is a vent pipe that goes to the top of the fuel tank. *(Paul Blackah)*

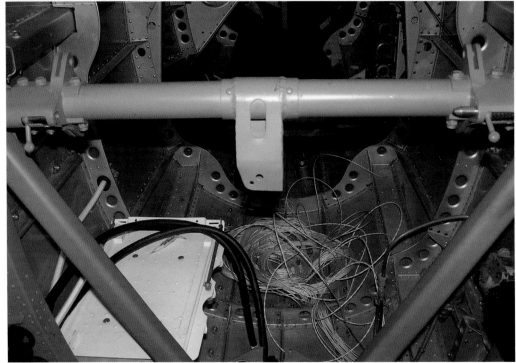

RIGHT Wiring waiting to be sorted. *(Paul Blackah)*

retractable tail leg, the hydraulic pipework that runs from the cockpit to the rear of the fuselage on its starboard side should be installed. The rudder and elevator trim systems on the port side of the fuselage should also be put in place. The fin unit, complete with tailplanes, should be bolted to the rear of the fuselage.

These systems are positioned prior to fitting the main elevator and rudder cable systems, because you need to have access to crawl inside the rear of the fuselage. This is not a job for a large person, as space is at a premium!

Moving into the cockpit area, the windscreen assembly, complete with armoured glass, should be installed, followed by the air pipes, hydraulic pipes and components (air bottles, undercarriage selector etc). These are fitted through to frame 5, which is the engine fireproof bulkhead, followed by the rudder pedals, instrument panel and control column. The throttle box and the engine controls, such as the CSU

control and the Teleflex conduit, are furnished through to the engine bay.

At the rear of the aircraft the tail leg, elevator and rudder can be fixed in, which now means that your fuselage is ready for the next stage, which is to prepare the wings for fitting. The wing systems are now positioned, including the wiring, aileron control cables, undercarriage

ABOVE Inside the rear fuselage are the tail leg and strut, also the rudder/elevator rear bellcranks and operating cables. Note, these cables are fitted in pairs; on later marks it changed to single cables. *(Paul Blackah)*

LEFT When fitting the undercarriage pintle and locking mechanism it is important to get the clearances correct. This may take several attempts, and some shimming, before they can then be locked in place. *(Paul Blackah)*

ABOVE Top wing spar bolts fitted. You are allowed to go oversize in four thou increments, seven times only. *(Paul Blackah)*

BELOW Wing fit in progress is made easy with the help of an overhead gantry and sling to support the wing. *(RAF BBMF)*

locking mechanism and pintle assembly. It is worth having the wings upside down in order to carry out this work. The locking mechanism and pintle assembly, together with the undercarriage leg, need to be checked at this stage for correct movement and clearances prior to the wings being put in place, because with the wings off there is more access to remove and adjust these components. Once you are happy with the fit and clearances of the leg it is then removed and the wings are turned into their correct position.

Other systems fitted at this stage include the pipework for the flap jacks, the flap jacks themselves and the spring assisting units for the flaps.

Now is time for the wings to be fitted. In order to do this the aircraft is 'levelled' and each wing is eased into place, checked for the correct alignment and dihedral (angle of wing to fuselage) and steadied with trestles. The trestles

support the wings, preventing any movement. The forward bolts are now ready for fitment. This is done by inserting plain metal dowels into three of the seven attachment holes. The remaining holes are then reamed one at a time to take the wing bolts, being heedful not to damage any of the holes, because if this occurs you must ream out to the next oversized bolt diameter. As you can only do this seven times, before a re-spar is needed, *great* care should be taken. After each hole is reamed and cleaned the wing bolt is inserted and tightened. This is carried out until all the bolts on each wing are in place. The wing trestles will remain in place until the aircraft is lowered off jacks.

After attending to the seven main wing bolts, the rear wing bolt is fitted. Connect up the aileron control cables from the wing to the control column in the fuselage, then the air pipes can be fastened to the fuselage attachments and any electrical plugs can be

ABOVE Bottom wing spar bolts fitted; the same applies as to the top wing spars. *(Paul Blackah)*

BELOW With the wings in place, dowels are inserted, and then each hole is reamed to accept the wing bolts. *(Paul Blackah)*

RIGHT Wing skin replacement being carried out on RW382.

(Paul Blackah)

BELOW TE311's aileron fit. Once rigged they will be removed, painted and balanced before final fit.

(Paul Blackah)

coupled up. Ailerons can be fitted and adjusted at the hinge points by winding them either in and out to get the right clearances. Once this is achieved the hinges are then wire locked so they cannot be moved.

The inboard and outboard flaps can be positioned and connected to the flap jack and the spring assisting assemblies. Care must be taken as the spring assembly needs to be gagged (locked in place) by means of a

ABOVE Flap jack and pipework in place.
(Paul Blackah))

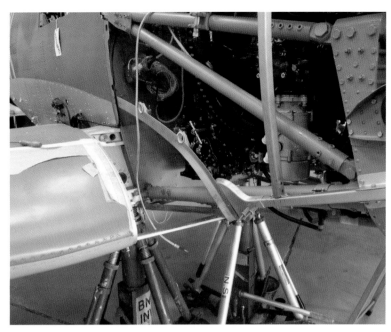

ABOVE Cowling rail framework fit in progress. Note the wing is only pinned at this stage and not bolted. *(Paul Blackah)*

split tube and jubilee clip. Once attached this gag can be removed and then the flaps will automatically close, so you need to be mindful not to trap your fingers!

The engine bearer can now be fitted to frame 5, by means of four taper bolts, if your engine is a Merlin. If it is a Griffon then the engine bearer is fixed to the engine prior to engine fit and your newly overhauled machine can be installed into the bearer or as a power plant to the airframe. Prior to fitting the engine you should install the hydraulic pump and compressor. In the case of a Griffon you should fasten the auxiliary gearbox

LEFT Side showing cowling framework in progress. *(Paul Blackah)*

RIGHT TD314's final assembly progressing. On the floor the top engine cowling is gripped together ready for a trial fit, and on the bench the engine air intake is having its filters examined.
(Paul Blackah)

BELOW GA (General Arrangement) drawings like this are a good source of information for what items are required to fit a system, in this case the engine breather drains.

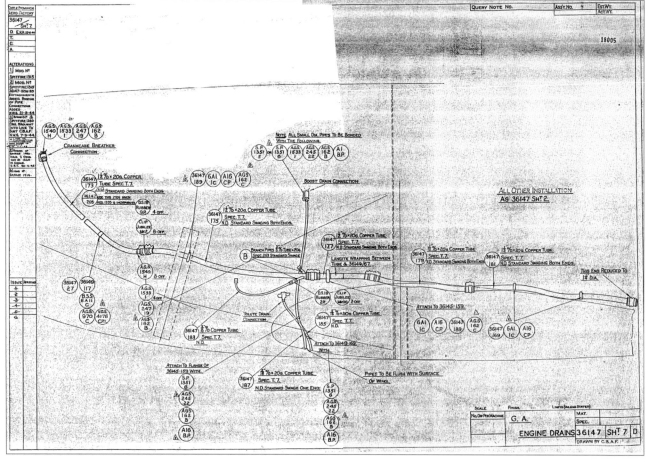

to frame 5, which has the hydraulic pump and compressor attached to it.

Once the engine is fitted, the engine controls can be connected (throttle linkages and CSU). Next, the oil system pipework and oil system breather pipework, along with the coolant system pipework, oil tank and coolant header tank can be installed. The hydraulic pump and air compressor are coupled to the relevant pipework.

To make these systems complete, the coolant radiators, oil cooler and intercooler radiator, if required, are incorporated into the wings. Once the oil and coolant systems are entire they are then filled to ensure there are no leaks. The coolant system, however, also has a pressure test carried out to make certain there is no seepage.

The time has now come to reattach the undercarriage legs. These are, again, inspected for the accurate clearances on fit. A hydraulic rig is connected to the aircraft and the undercarriage is manually pumped up to

ABOVE Close-up of the coolant system pipe, complete with electrical temp bulb. *(Paul Blackah)*

BELOW Oil system drawing for a Packard Merlin 266. This is where you have to be careful as the pipework for the 266 installation is different to the Merlin 60 series, but the drawing numbers are similar.

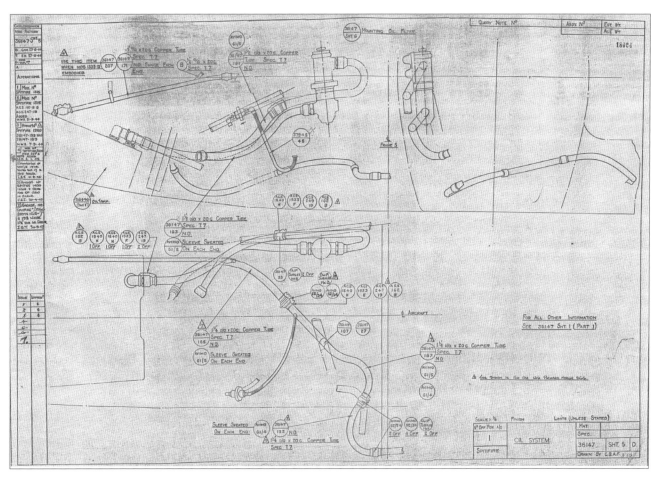

ABOVE Coolant and oil pipes installed. *(Paul Blackah)*

ABOVE The fuel vent system fitted. *(Paul Blackah)*

ABOVE Cowling rails complete; oil, coolant pipes and airbox are fitted. *(Paul Blackah)*

ABOVE Undercarriage leg fit under way. Once fitted the leg is checked for clearances. They should be between 2 and 12 thou on the pintle; this allows the leg to move freely. *(RAF BBMF)*

LEFT Undercarriage leg and door fitted. The flexible hose will connect to the brake unit when in position. *(Paul Blackah)*

BELOW Bottom fuel tank fitted; the gap at the back allows a pipe from the top tank to connect to the bottom tank. The tank is held in place by four cables that are locked into the green fittings. *(Paul Blackah)*

check that it moves correctly. Once the legs are retracted the system is then hand pumped up to a pressure of 1,150psi and the undercarriage selector should click into idle. All the pipework should be examined for leaks. The gear then selected down and locked.

Next, the lower fuel tank is fitted, but not secured in place, as a further retraction of the undercarriage is required to ensure that the undercarriage jack pipework does not foul on the lower tank. If it does, the tank is removed, the pipework is adjusted and the tank is replaced, and the system is checked again.

The top fuel tank is fitted and connected to the lower tank and all fuel system pipework is installed from the tanks to the engine.

A series of functional tests are carried out, as detailed in the Aircraft Functional Tests section (see below). Some are carried out at this point in the build; however, the compass swing test requires the aircraft to be complete.

Finally, fit the wing to fuselage filet panels and the engine cowlings: side, top and lower, and the radiator fairings. Wing and fuselage access panels can be fixed once the functional tests have been completed.

The last major component to go on is the

LEFT New leading edge panel skins; they will require trimming to fit prior to assembly. *(Paul Blackah)*

ABOVE AND LEFT Rear fuselage fillet panel; this comes oversized and requires trimming to fit. *(Paul Blackah)*

RIGHT **Lower engine cowling being assembled on the aircraft. This is done so that all the fasteners will line up with their respective receptacles, ensuring the panel fits correctly.** *(Paul Blackah)*

propeller. The spinner will not be added until after the first engine ground run; this is done so that the propeller can be leak inspected for leaks.

Aircraft Functional Tests

Undercarriage functionals

The aircraft must be jacked and trestled and a hydraulic rig connected to carry out the functional tests. The hydraulic rig is attached to two test points on the hydraulic pump. The hydraulic reservoir should be examined to make sure the fluid is at the correct level, which is done with the undercarriage legs in the down position; the oil level should just be touching the dipstick in the hydraulic reservoir.

Aircraft power should be switched on, using either the aircraft battery or a ground power unit plugged into the plane. Looking at the instrument panel there should be a green light illuminated ON, which indicates that the undercarriage legs are in the down position. With someone in the cockpit to operate the undercarriage selector, another person to operate the hydraulic rig and a safety man to watch the undercarriage go up and down – ensuring that there are no obstacles to prevent the gear from functioning – you are ready to begin the procedure.

The hydraulic rig is started up and then the person in the cockpit selects UP using the undercarriage selector. This operation rotates the port and starboard undercarriage locking mechanism plungers by moving cables and chains that are attached to the selector. At the same time, in operating the selector handle, hydraulic pressure goes to the upside of the jack, thus making the legs move upwards. The

BELOW **With the undercarriage leg up, the door is checked for correct fit.** *(Paul Blackah)*

green light goes out during travel and a red light comes on when the undercarriage is in the locked UP position. Once the UP mode is achieved, a cut-out valve in the undercarriage selector will relieve the hydraulic pressure. This cut-out operates around 1,150psi. This makes the undercarriage selector indicator go from UP to IDLE.

The person in the cockpit is told to remove his hand from the selector while the safety man checks that the legs are in the UP position and that the undercarriage doors are fitted to the correct profile to the wing.

The legs are now put into DOWN. The undercarriage selector is moved forwards to energise the hydraulic pressure for 1–2 seconds; this lifts the legs off the locks so that when the lever is moved into the DOWN position the plungers can rotate. The gear will then lower. The red light goes out, the gear travels and the green light comes on when the gear is locked down. The cut-out operates again and the selector indicator goes from DOWN to IDLE. This test is carried out several times to ensure that the system works correctly, with no leaks from any of the system components.

The next stage is to check the emergency blow-down system. This is a backup to get the undercarriage down in the event of hydraulic failure. It works by forcing air into the retraction jacks in order to push the undercarriage into the locked-down position. To test the blow-down system the undercarriage is selected to UP and the hydraulic rig is switched off. To simulate the loss of hydraulics and the aircraft inverting, a person on each undercarriage leg pushes the legs up off the locks and then DOWN is selected. The legs are allowed to free-fall and then the emergency blow-down bottle lever is moved forward, which lets air into the system to push the jacks into the fully locked and down position. During this operation the red light will go off when selected and when the gear is locked down the green light will come on. The undercarriage selector, however, will not move from DOWN into IDLE, because there is insufficient pressure – less than 1,150psi – to do this. The emergency blow-down bottle handle is reset and a bucket or drip tray is placed under the hydraulic vent pipe to capture any expelled oil.

To reset the oil level after this test, the aircraft is left for approximately 15–20 minutes to allow the air pressure to dissipate and then the hydraulic level should be re-established by refilling the reservoir and initiating several undercarriage cycles to expel any remaining air. Once the undercarriage is operating smoothly, and the level is correct, this operation is complete. The final job is to recharge the air bottle on the blow-down system so that it is ready for use if required.

Fuel calibration

This is carried out to ensure that an accurate reading is being given by the aircraft's fuel gauge. On most Spitfires, only the bottom gauge indicates. The tail of the aircraft is placed on a rear trestle and adjusted so that the aircraft is in the 'straight and level' position – as it would be during flight.

The system is then filled and subsequently drained into calibrated bins. This gives an accurate reading of the amount of fuel that the aircraft can hold. If required, the fuel sender can be adjusted, which gives a reading to the gauge of how much fuel is left in the tank; for example, informing the ground crew, as part of this calibration, that there remains approximately 1 gallon left when it is reading zero. This errs on the side of caution as you would not want the gauge to read 5 gallons, for instance, when in fact it is empty.

When planning a trip a pilot should allow for a reserve of fuel – approximately 10 gallons – so that if diverted due to weather, it would be easy to make it to another airfield. Or in the event of any problems occurring – such as the undercarriage not locking down properly – there would be sufficient fuel in the tank for circling the airfield in order to resolve the problem. So knowing that your system is correctly calibrated helps enormously when organising the length and time of your trips.

Flying control range of movements

Once all the flying controls are fitted and all the control cables and operating rods are in place, the next step is to ensure that all the controls are adjusted to give the correct range of movements. The range of movements for the aircraft can be found in the relevant AP1565, Vol I, for the mark of aircraft that is being restored.

The aircraft needs to be in the rigging position (on jacks and with the fuselage level in both axes) before beginning. For the ailerons a special rigging tool is required, the dimensions of which are, again, laid down in the aircraft manual, Vol I. This is used to make certain that the bellcranks in the wing are set to the right position when the cables are correctly tensioned. A clinometer or ruler is used to measure the range of movements and a cable tensiometer is used to check the flying control cable tensions. Tensions should be inspected at an approximate temperature of 15°C. If it's done when the weather is too cold then the cables could be too slack.

The ailerons are rigged so that when they are in the neutral position they are both 3/8in down from the wing trailing edge, which is called aileron droop. This can be altered to achieve the correct position by adjusting the input rod to the aileron, not by adjusting the cables to the bellcrank, as this will throw out the bellcrank in relation to the rigging tool. Once the droop is

set and the tensions are correct, the range of movement can be checked.

The elevator and the rudder are set by making sure that the horn of the flying controls is level with the tailplane and fin. The cables are tensioned and if any alteration is required to bring the controls into line, this will be done by tweaking the input rod to the control. The up and down ranges are then measured on the elevator and the left and right on the rudder. Depending again on which mark of Spitfire, the rudder range can vary due to the different sizes of rudders.

Rudder and elevator trim are checked in the same way, although it should be noted that there are no laid down cable tensions for these systems; they are tensioned by feel and how the trim wheels are smooth and free to operate. If too stiff then the tensions are too tight.

Electrical checks

Once the aircraft has been rewired all the systems need to be examined to ensure

BELOW Inside the cockpit of TE311 complete with modern GPS/radio unit. *(Crown Copyright/RAF Coningsby)*

that they are earthed properly. The fuses are then removed and each system is inspected for shorts to earth. The external power is subsequently connected and each system has its fuse fitted and is tested for correct working, for example navigation lights. Switch on the system and you should have two wingtip lights and a tail light. If they don't work as they should, and the bulbs are known to be functional, then the wiring must be checked again for correct orientation, in accordance with the system diagrams. This is carried out for every system.

Electrical checks are also instigated during engine ground runs; these tests ensure that the generator and the voltage regulator are working as they should. If the generator is not producing enough power – 24 volts – the voltage regulator is adjusted to give the correct voltage.

The radios and IFF, if fitted, are also scrutinised by making certain that all communication channels are open and working well.

Independent checks (on systems)

Independent, or duplicate inspections, are carried out on the undercarriage, brakes, flying controls, engine controls and pitot static systems when the system has been disturbed or, in our case, when the system has been restored and rebuilt. These checks are done by a person who has *not* worked on these systems. This ensures that they are checked by a 'fresh' pair of eyes. This person will be looking at any locking such as split pins and wire locking, correct assembly in accordance with drawing and diagrams, and will also investigate tensions and range of movements.

After a successful examination, this person will then sign this work off. If not satisfied with, for example, the locking of a component, he will insist that it is corrected before it is signed off.

Pneumatic functionals

These inspections are conducted on the aircraft air system and will include brakes and flaps. This system, which comprises two air cylinders, is charged to 300psi. All pipelines are 'snooped' for leaks, which involves using a mild liquid detergent that, when sprayed on the union, will bubble up if there is a leak present. The other way to check for leaks is to look at the main

system gauge and if it goes down rapidly there is obviously a major seepage in the system.

To test the brakes the aircraft should, ideally, be on jacks. If you have spare brake drums then the wheels should be removed and the brake drums placed over the brake unit. With the brake lever applied, air inflates the brake bag of the brake unit, which pushes the brake pads against the drum. The drum should then not rotate. The brake gauge is checked for the correct pressure and again this will depend on the mark of Spitfire as to pressure required. If the bag is leaking, for example on the port side, the port side brake gauge needle will go down. You can look inside the brake unit using 'snoop' and unions can be tightened if required. If the bag is leaking it will require replacing as these cannot be repaired.

The check for differential braking is performed with the brakes in the ON position. The rudder is then moved fully one way, the brake unit corresponding to the rudder movement is then off while the other stays on. The rudder is then rotated the other way and again the corresponding brake unit should be on and the other off as above. Drawing the rudder back to neutral brings both brake units on. The brake lever is then released and both units should then be off. If at any time the brake gauge does not return to zero, the brake cable may require adjusting or, if this does not work, the BCV (brake control valve) may be faulty and need replacing.

To functionally test the flaps, make sure the air system is fully charged and the flaps are selected with the flap selector lever on the instrument panel. The flaps then go fully down together and are measured for their range of movement. This can be adjusted on the eye end of the flap jack; however, when they are fully up they should be flush with the trailing edge of the wing.

The flaps are then selected UP, the air dissipates from the jack and a spring-loaded unit on each flap pulls them up together. The jacks are not allowed to leak and any asymmetric movement should not be allowed.

Pitot static checks

This inspection is carried out to monitor the operation of the Air Speed Indicator (ASI), altimeter and the Rate of Climb indicator. A test set is connected to the pressure head, which is located under the port wing. There are two tests: one is a sense check and the other is a leak check.

The sense check is carried out to test the ASI. The test set is established at 130 knots and the ASI is examined for a positive indication. The altimeter and the Rate of Climb indicator should have not moved.

The leak check is then carried out by pumping air pressure into the system. The ASI should not move; however, on the altimeter the indication increases to simulate the altitude of the aircraft. The Rate of Climb indicator shows a positive display. If you don't get these readings there is obviously a leak in the pipeline and all pipes and connections should be investigated to find the leak in question by using snoop.

Once these tests are completed the test set is removed.

Compass swing

This is one of the last tasks, as the aircraft needs to complete. The compass swing is conducted in an area on the airfield designated for this task, where the earth's magnetic field is free from all external interference, meaning that there are no metal pipes etc situated in the immediate locality.

Position the aircraft on the compass pan, on the required heading according to the aircraft

RIGHT Carrying out a compass swing. The compass on the tripod is checking the aircraft's compass for accuracy at set headings. *(RAF BBMF)*

compass and then take the bearing of its fore and aft lines by means of the datum instrument. This is then carried out on the main compass headings: north, south, east and west, followed by north-east, north-west, south-east and south-west.

Any deviations from the aircraft compass t o the datum instrument are plotted on a compass correction card, so that when in flight the pilot can refer to the card to obtain an accurate reading.

Painting your aircraft

This is one process that you will definitely need an outside company for. It needs specialist equipment, an eye for detail and knowledge of the various paint colours that will match the original wartime colours as near as possible.

Colour scheme – researching known history

Once your aircraft is assembled the final task is to have her painted up in whatever colour scheme you desire; after all, it is your aircraft. Initial choice of scheme is dependent on whether, after researching your particular aircraft's history, you want the paint scheme to represent one of the units that the aircraft originally operated with.

Another option is to paint the aircraft in a colour scheme representing another Spitfire that perhaps has a more interesting history than yours, or was flown by a well-known fighter ace. RAF BBMF change the colour schemes on their aircraft relatively frequently to represent an individual or squadron aircraft; however, it is to be noted that BBMF now always ensure that the paint scheme is correct to the mark of Spitfire, something that the purist enthusiast would appreciate.

Once you've chosen your squadron, whether it be the aircraft's original or another, your research can begin. Squadron records can be accessed through the internet; a simple google search can reveal much information. What you really need are photographs of the aircraft that you wish to represent, preferably as many as possible showing both sides of the aircraft. RAF BBMF has often found squadron associations

and internet aircraft forums very cooperative and useful as well as aviation historians and enthusiasts with their own private collections of photographs.

It is to be noted that the Spitfire paint colours themselves did alter over the course of the years; for example, the early marks were dark green and dark earth camouflage for top surfaces and white and black or sky or duck egg blue under-surfaces, changing to dark green and ocean grey for the top surfaces and medium sea grey for the underside on later marks. Some post-war/later marks went on to being all over silver in appearance.

Roundel, fin flashes and squadron codes also had variations in size and some colour changes over the different marks. All this attention to detail will ensure that the finished article will be as accurate as possible.

Vintage Fabrics is a company that not only conducts restoration work on historic aircraft, but also specialises in paint schemes. Clive Denney filled us in on the company and the process.

Based at Audley End airfield in Essex, Vintage Fabrics is a fully approved CAA A8-20 organisation, approval number DA1/9934/09, which carries out full restoration to flying condition and maintenance on all types of historic aircraft. It is well known for its quality fabric re-covers, but it also does a lot of painting work.

Formed in 1986 by Clive and Linda Denney in a small workshop in Rayne, near Braintree in Essex, carrying out re-covers on MOD Chipmunks at Stansted (60 in all), the business has gone from strength to strength.

The company amalgamated in 1988 with Tim Routsis to form Historic Flying Ltd and moved to a purpose-built hangar at Audley End. This started the love affair with anything Spitfire. In 1997 Historic Flying was passed on to a new

ABOVE Fresh from the spray shop, AB910 in its 303 Squadron markings. This was painted by Clive Denney of Vintage Fabrics. *(Paul Blackah)*

LEFT A pair of newly painted wings from a static Mark 21. *(Clive Denney)*

BELOW TD314 codes after painting and with masking tape removed. *(Clive Denney)*

owner and Vintage Fabrics was resurrected to its present form and relocated to workshops at Earls Colne. Another move was required when the workshops at Earls Colne were shut down, and so the company transferred to the Braintree area. Clive now takes up the story:

In 2007 Vintage Fabrics moved back to Audley End to Historic Flying Ltd's original hangar and has remained there to this day. Pete Wood joined the team as a partner and plays a pivotal role in the company. The year 2012 saw a massive extension to the hangar as space was getting tight. Spitfires are still coming in and out at Audley End on a regular basis, so we have come almost full circle.

Having been involved in the restoration of various Spitfires for the last 25 years, the one question which keeps being asked is 'How do you go about painting a Spitfire?'

In the very early days it was a very daunting prospect; it was all too easy to ruin a great restoration with a bad paint job, likewise you could transform a bad restoration with a good paint job.

So where do you start? Research nowadays has been done a million times by so-called experts, but the biggest source of information now is the scale-model world. There are books in their hundreds referring to this scheme and that scheme. Paint colours need little or no research, the bottom line is that British wartime aircraft used the British Standard scheme, which is still going strong today. So, as long as you have the BS number (usually a BS381C code) you can order your paint and have it the next day. Simple!

If you are lucky you may have a factory drawing which will give you the size and style of the camouflage pattern, either A or B scheme, one being a mirror image of the other. Also on the drawing are all the markings and stencils required for the whole aircraft so this drawing is a must for absolute accuracy.

The next step is to study photos of the period: all Spitfires started life with a standard camouflage, but due to repairs through damage or a change of operational theatre the colours, styles and quality would change. A Spitfire wasn't grounded just because the right shade of paint wasn't in the stores, so field variations were inevitable. Period photos help to establish the changes but are subject to interpretation. A good photo of the subject is worth a hundred opinions.

A lot of Spitfires carried distinctive personal artwork. This is a major problem when trying to identify colours from a period black and white photo. Usually bright colours were used – reds, whites, yellows, blues etc. Sometimes it is possible to check against roundel colours for shade variations, sometimes the original pilot can tell you, sometimes a colour photo or even the original artwork is available, but this is rare. We were able to replicate Wing Commander Ian Gleed's cat (Figaro) on the BBMF Spitfire Mark V, AB910, from the original panel taken from the crash at the time; this was held at the RAF Museum, and for us this was a finisher's dream.

A Spitfire, although small in size, is impractical to try to paint all in one go. Keeping the paint wet is a major issue; also not tying yourself up in the spray hose is another. Hopefully you will be approaching a so-called blank canvas, ie a paint-stripped aircraft.

Following paint stripping, the aircraft will need a thorough clean. The last thing you want is paint stripper under fresh paint. Once thoroughly clean the aircraft is masked ready to prime. Priming is done in two stages: first an acid etch, followed by an epoxy two-part primer. Once dry the primer can be nibbed off (lightly rubbed down), recleaned and you are ready to top coat.

The obvious way is to break it down into sections. The underside can be done in one go because it is just one colour – either Sky Type S or Medium Sea Grey or possibly Azure Blue for Mediterranean schemes. Either way you are on your back working hard, hopefully with someone feeding you the airline to stop you getting snagged. Air-fed masks are used at all times: they are vital but can be cumbersome.

Once the underside is completed this is left overnight to dry.

The next stage is the camouflage. This needs to be carefully planned. I always do the fuselage first, and when fully dry, paint the wings and tailplane. All roundels and fin flashes are masked out before the camouflage

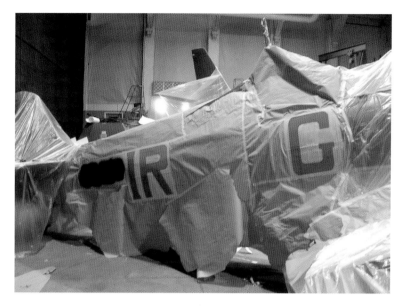

is applied. All items that are removable but need camouflage are painted separately, ie cowlings, flying controls etc. These require careful marking out: nothing looks worse than misaligned camouflage.

Again, once all is dry you apply all your roundels, squadron codes, serial numbers and stencils; this equates to putting the decals on your model – the so-called finishing touch. You are now near the end – de-mask your aircraft and stand back. You need to check for any bleed through or pulled paint – fortunately a rare occurrence these days. There it is, your fresh out-of-the-box-looking Spitfire. All it needs now is a few oil streaks, some exhaust staining and hopefully you will have yourself an authentic-

ABOVE This gives an idea of how much paper and tape is used just for code letters.
(Clive Denney)

LEFT Masking the squadron codes prior to painting.
(Clive Denney)

RIGHT Squadron
codes FX–P in the
process of being
masked. (Clive Denney)

looking aircraft. Spitfires, or in fact any aircraft that flies, never stay pristine for long – they develop a patina very quickly. So, in answer to the original question – 'What does it take to paint a Spitfire?' – I think firstly passion for the subject, a small amount of research, the right equipment to do the job, the right team and the rest is easy.

We owe a tremendous amount to the modelling world for all their research; they used to say if it's good enough for the real thing it's good enough for the model. I would say it's more like the other way round.

In my time we have had the privilege of painting the following flying Spitfires:

RW382, Mark XVI (painted 1989 and 2011)
RW386, Mark XVI
TD248, Mark XVI
TE566, Mark IX
AR614, Mark V
EP120, Mark V
BM597, Mark V
AB910, Mark V (painted)
NH799, Mark XIV
PM631, Mark XIX
TP280, MarK XVIII
SM832, Mark XIV
NH637, Mark IX two-seat
TD314, Mark IX
LA255, Mark XXI
X4650, Mark I
LZ842, Mark IX
SM969, Mark XVIII
PV202, Mark IX 2 seat
PP972, Seafire III
SM845, Mark XIV (fuselage only)
TE311, Mark XVI (fuselage only)
Plus two full-scale replicas:
BBMF, Mark I (Molly), now on show at
    Duxford
MH434 (replica), Breitling HQ in
    Switzerland

The process described in this chapter applies to all the warbird paint schemes Vintage Fabrics has carried out over the years. We will leave all the Hurricanes, Mosquitoes, Bf109s and Luftwaffe aircraft (various) for another book!

BELOW Ballast
weights are provided
in the rear fuselage
to keep the aircraft's
CoG within limits.
(Paul Blackah)

Weighing the aircraft

The very last job on the rebuild is to weigh the aircraft. This needs to be done to make sure that the aircraft's centre of gravity (CoG) is in the correct position. The main wheels are placed on scales and the fuselage is lifted into the flying position; a series of calculations then establishes the weight of the aircraft and the position of the CoG. If the CoG is too far forward, there is provision (on a Merlin Spitfire) in the fin unit, above the tail leg, to fit ballast weights on a bar assembly to correct it. Most, if not all, Spitfires achieve the correct CoG by only using three or four of these weights.

In a Griffon Spitfire, the ballast weights are higher up in the fin unit and provision for extra weight is located just inside the rear fuselage hatch on the starboard side where up to an extra 8 x 17½lb lead weights can be fitted if required.

ABOVE The scales are set to zero prior to the aircraft being pushed on to them for weighing. *(Paul Blackah)*

BELOW With the aircraft on the weighing scales it is lifted into the rigging position to work out the centre of gravity. *(Paul Blackah)*

Chapter Eight

Flight and maintenance

Your aircraft is fully assembled, engine tested and almost ready for flight. However there are still the formalities to take care of. A final check of the paperwork is essential at this stage, and any issues that have been raised by the CAA inspectors now have to be addressed before an air test can be undertaken. Consideration should be given to the maintenance of the aircraft as well as who will be piloting it, but at last your dream is becoming a reality.

OPPOSITE TE311 in the air after an 11-year restoration.
(Keith Wilson)

CAA inspections and paperwork

So your aircraft is complete and looks the part, with just the final hurdle to be overcome – the inevitable paperwork!

One of the most important aspects of your restoration project is the paperwork. It is essential that any item that is purchased or manufactured for your Spitfire meets certain requirements. You need to know that it has arrived with the correct paperwork. This paperwork will tell you that it is fit to be used. In the case of a manufactured item it should tell you the material it has been made from, what drawings it has been manufactured in accordance with, even down to what treatments the material has had; for example, heat treatment, any NDT carried out etc. This is all laid out on a Certificate of Conformity, which is provided by the company that has produced it.

Ideally, for ease of a quality audit, this company should be CAA authorised to produce and manufacture items for this aircraft type. These businesses are themselves audited by the CAA to ensure that they maintain the correct standards to enable them to manufacture components. If standards lapse then a company may not be able to renew its accreditation.

If you have components manufactured from a non-CAA accredited firm, as long as you have a CAA-licensed engineer on site, rebuilding your aircraft, he can make the decision on whether that item is fit for use.

This process also applies for parts purchased rather than manufactured and, again, if you are buying spares from ebay or the internet, for example, then it is down to your licensed engineer to ensure that they are fit for purpose, because they will probably not come with any paperwork. As long as you can prove that the items are what they are said to be, by part numbers etc, then they will be deemed suitable.

On RAF BBMF any company manufacturing spares has to etch the part number on the item as well as their identification code; for instance, SAE stamped on an item means it is manufactured by Supermarine Engineering. The part number will be the same as the original item number, as indicated by original drawings. This enables the part to be traced back to source should a problem arise.

The same rules apply if you are using a firm to restore the airframe and engine. Ideally they should be approved CAA organisations. At the time of writing, these companies will come under the A8-21 system, although this system will supposedly be changing in the near future.

The A8-21 system of accreditation is broken down into the following groups:

A2 suppliers – These can manufacture components and assemblies, so will include companies such as Airframe Assemblies and Supermarine Engineering.
E4/M5 – These businesses are responsible for the restoration, airworthiness control and maintenance of aircraft. They are companies such as Retro Track and Air, ARCO and Airframe Assemblies.
M3 – These are companies that can perform maintenance checks on aircraft that do not exceed 2,730kg, and include Air Leasing Ltd, who maintain a two-seater Spitfire, and ARCO at Duxford who also maintain Spitfires.

There are other categories, but those above are the main ones that you should look for when choosing which companies will help you with your project.

Throughout your restoration you should involve the CAA, so that they can stage-check the project to ensure that all is correct at every major juncture. What you *don't* want to happen is to complete the project only to find the CAA inspector needs to see something that requires you to strip the aircraft out again.

Any deviation from the original build is classed as a modification, and an approval to embody this modification, regardless of its size, should be cleared through the CAA before proceeding. The CAA is basically the aviation equivalent of the planning authority at the local council. Build something unauthorised and you will be required to pull it down!

This process is one of the most important steps on your route to completion of your project and, as such, care must be taken when preparing the paperwork ready for examination by the CAA. By way of example, we have included opposite a fictitious Airworthiness Approval Note (AAN), based on an imaginary aircraft. The Airworthiness Note would be submitted to the CAA after air testing, but before being given clearance to fly.

Airworthiness Approval Note No 12345

Applicant	Joe Bloggs Ltd
Aircraft type	Vickers Supermarine Spitfire Mark XVI
Registration No	G-BBMF constructor's number CB-AF-12345 (Ex-ZA123 (ex-service number))
Operator	Bloggs Aviation
Installer	
Design organisation	Bloggs Aviation (E4 approval AB/1234567/13)
Certificate category	Permit to fly
Modification No	
Modification title	To approve Spitfire Mark XVI registered G-BBMF for issue of a permit to fly

Introduction

This Spitfire Mark XVI was manufactured at the Castle Bromwich Aircraft Factory against a contract number Air/1234 and delivered to the Royal Air Force in 1945. The works serial number CB-AF-12345 and military serial number ZA123 were allocated. After an operational career it was retired to gate guard duties in 1954. It was removed from gate guard duties and placed into storage in 1970.

In 2001 it was purchased by Bloggs Aviation where restoration work began.

This AAN is to record approval for the issue of a UK permit to fly.

Aircraft build standard/description

The Spitfire Mark XVI is a single-seat, low-wing monoplane fighter, powered by a Packard Merlin 266 engine, driving a four-blade Dowty Rotol constant-speed propeller. This aircraft is a low-back variant with clipped wings. Several modifications have been installed on this aircraft and these are detailed in section 5.1.2.3. below.

Airframe

The airframe maintenance manuals are Air Ministry publications AP1565K and L series.

Mainplane

The mainplanes incorporate a light alloy skin, with a main D-spar, with auxiliary rear spar and ribs, secured onto the fuselage by stub wing spars booms. The main undercarriage retracts hydraulically outboard into the wing forward of the radiators.

The fuselage stub spars have been replaced with items manufactured from L102. This material change has been reviewed and accepted by CAA Engineering Department (Structures Branch). Email dated 1 April 2008 refers.

The wing spar booms have been replaced with L105 tubes, heat treated at Senior Heat Treatments Ltd to meet the L63 specification. These tubes meet DTD 273 specification so compliance with MPD 1995-092 (paragraph i) is achieved and additional aerobatic restrictions are not required. CAA Engineering Department (Structures Branch) email dated 1 April 2008 refers.

Fuselage

The semi-monocoque fuselage includes four main longerons plus one dorsal longeron from cockpit to tail, oval U-shape frames and intercostal stiffeners, the whole being rivetted together.

The Merlin engine is supported on a tubular frame, which is attached directly to the fuselage top longerons and to the lower longerons. The engine bearer has been refurbished. Applicant's work pack 101 refers.

Empennage and controls

The tail section of the fuselage is a separate unit with integral fin, bolted to the main structure. The tailplane is made in halves, which are then fitted to the tail section. The rudder and elevator is of metal construction with fabric covering. Ailerons are metal covered and trim tabs are fitted to the rudder and elevator only. Pneumatic-operated split flaps are incorporated. Control runs consist of high-tensile cables and levers.

The fin and tailplane were in poor condition and were overhauled by Airframe Assemblies, Sandown, Isle of Wight. All control cables have been replaced by cables manufactured to the original drawings/specification by Bruntons of Musselburgh. Bearings, rods, levers, Teleflex, control column and rudder pedals have been inspected and overhauled or replaced in accordance with manufacturer's drawings as required.

Powerplant

Engine

The original Packard Merlin 266 serial number V30036 has been overhauled by Retro Track and Air UK (CAA approval DAI/9631/97) in 2008. The engine was completely stripped and rebuilt in accordance with AP2616 and was installed in the airframe for testing. The engine has been run for a period of three hours and has been released for a life of 500 hours or 12 years, whichever comes first. The carburettor and magnetos were overhauled as part of the same work package.

Propeller

The propeller is a four-blade constant-speed Dowty Rotol R/4F5, serial number 3456, and was overhauled by Skycraft Ltd and has been released for 350 hours or 6 years. The propeller blades are replacement Hoffmann items.

Fuel system

The fuel system consists of the original forward fuselage 48-gallon (top) and 48-gallon (bottom) tanks. An electric boost pump, which has been overhauled by Kearsey Aviation is fitted.

The aircraft has had an ability to carry a range of jettisonable fuel tanks under the fuselage for ferry purposes. These jettisonable tanks are not fitted at permit issue and are therefore not approved by this AAN.

Cooling system

A radiator is located under each side of the mainplane. The starboard radiator fairing houses one main coolant radiator and an intercooler radiator. The port fairing houses the other main coolant radiator and the oil cooler. Pneumatically operated thermostatically controlled flaps regulate the flow through these radiators. A manual override facility to operate these flaps is installed and all parts of the coolant system have been stripped or replaced, rebuilt and pressure tested.

Oil system

The oil tank has been rebuilt and the oil cooler overhauled. All components have been stripped and tested.

Starting

The engine is fitted with an electric starter motor, which has been fully overhauled.

Systems

Hydraulics

The hydraulic system operates the undercarriage and the pressure is generated by a pressure-driven pump. All components have been serviced and pipelines replaced as required.

Pneumatic system

The pneumatic system is supplied with compressed air from two storage bottles and pressure is maintained by an engine-driven compressor. This system operates the split flaps, radiator flaps and the main wheel brakes. The complete system has been serviced and pipelines replaced as required.

Electrical system

The aircraft is fitted with a 24V electrical system with a generator, voltage regulator and aircraft battery fitted behind frame 11. (See applicant's modification list.) Power is controlled through a ground/flight switch and an external power connector is incorporated.

Instruments

All instruments are replacement items (non-radioactive) where possible and have been serviced and calibrated.

Undercarriage

This comprises of two cantilever struts, retracting outboard into the mainplanes. The tail leg is fixed. New wheels and tyres have been fitted. (See applicant's modifications list.)

For emergency lowering a compressed nitrogen blow-down system has been installed, again see applicant's modification list.

Safety harness

A ZB-type harness is fitted and has been given a 12-month life.

Windscreen de-icing

This is not fitted to this aircraft.

Oxygen system

The oxygen regulator is fitted, as are the oxygen bottles, but this system is no longer in use.

Approval procedures

The aircraft approval has been carried out in accordance with BCAR A3-7.

Basis of approval

CAA approval basis for this aircraft

The design code used as a basis for service acceptance was the Air Ministry's specifications and Supermarine type 361. Approval for the aircraft is based on previous satisfactory experience together with published modifications and inspections. Any new work has been examined against the requirements of BCAR Section K.

CAA design requirements for permit issue

Generic Requirement 6 of CAP 747.
Any installed equipment, for which the Air Navigation Order requires approval, must be approved by the CAA.

Environmental requirements

Aeroplane noise regulations 1999.

Design requirements associated with operational approvals

None applicable.

Compliance with the basis of approval

Compliance with the approval basis for the aircraft

Modifications and inspections have been introduced under three headings as follows:
Those listed in the AP 1565W, Vol 2
Those subsequently found necessary by the RAF
Those generated by the applicant.

AP 1565W modifications

The AP 1565W, Vol 2, lists those modifications applicable to the Spitfire. The applicability of these modifications has been assessed and those considered relevant to the airworthiness of the aircraft have been embodied. The applicant has provided modification statement 'Spitfire ZA123/G-BBMF Modification List', which confirms a satisfactory modification state of the aircraft.

Modifications and inspections subsequently found necessary by the RAF

The RAF in the course of their continued operation of the Spitfire, found the following modification necessary and these are incorporated in accordance with Spitfire Aircraft Service Instructions, HQ Home Command, RAF, 29 August 1951 and are as follows:

STI/SPIT/17	Fairey fasteners incorrectly made
STI/SPIT/19	Exhaust stubs, internal blistering
STI/SPIT/51/51a	Fairey sockets, incorrect type
STI/SPIT/62	Safety thread on canopy jettison
STI/SPIT/72	Oleo upper torsion link cracking
STI/SPIT/73	Oleo torsion links fouling on lugs
STI/SPIT/75	Elevator control rod end socket

The applicant has confirmed, in the design report, dated 1 April 2008, that the modifications applicable to Spitfire G-BBMF have been addressed.

Battle of Britain Flight inspections

As a result of experience gained by the Battle of Britain Memorial Flight, certain radiological inspections are considered to be necessary before accepting an old aeroplane for the issue of a permit to fly. This information is contained in AP 101B-001-5G and covers engine bearer assembly, fuselage longerons, steel bracing tubes housed within the fuselage, forward upper longerons, ailerons, elevators, rudder, frame 11 cross braces and spar booms.

The applicant has confirmed that these examinations have been carried out where applicable, also that stub axles, undercarriage pintles and undercarriage locking mechanism eye bolts were checked using NDT and found to be satisfactory.

Applicant's modifications

The following modifications have been incorporated into this aircraft:

RAF/SEM/SPIT/01	To introduce alternative blow-down bottle
MOD/BLOGGS/SPIT/01	Introduce stainless steel fire wall
MOD/BLOGGS/SPIT/02	Introduce tubeless wheels
MOD/BLOGGS/SPIT/03	Introduce metal seat
MOD/BLOGGS/SPIT/04	Introduce improved oil filtration.

The applicant's modification leaflets have been reviewed and accepted by the CAA.

Compliance with design requirements for permit to fly

The applicant's E4 report dated 1 April 2008 confirms that a starter-engaged warning light and a low-volt warning light are installed.

The following avionic equipment is fitted:
Garmin radio/GPS unit
Becker IFF unit.

Compliance with environmental requirements

As this aircraft operates on a permit to fly, it is exempt from the requirements of the noise order.

Required manuals and other documents including mandatory placards

Flight manual

The applicant has prepared a set of pilot's notes based on the AP1565J and L, specifically for G-BBMF.

Placards

Placards are to be installed for the following limitations:
Aerobatic limitations
Airspeed limitations
Engine limitations
No smoking.

BELOW The instrument panel with the placarding in place: limitations, maximum weight and aircraft registration – G-PMNF. *(Paul Blackah)*

Weight and balance

The aircraft has been weighed; Loadmaster's report ref. 25/03/2008 and a new weight and CoG schedule completed. CoG datum is within limits laid down in the AP1565J and L.

Maintenance

The aircraft is to be maintained in accordance with the RAF maintenance schedule 5A1, issued 2006. The relevant manuals, as below, cover the airframe and engine:

AP1565 series, Vols 1–3   For Spitfire Marks IX and XVI

AP1590 series, Vols 1–3   For Rolls-Royce Merlin engines
AP2616 series   For Packard Merlin 266

Conditions affecting this approval

In the absence of more complete manufacturers' test data a safety factor of 0.9 (in accordance with the BCAR K7.2) has been applied to the maximum demonstrated flight speed to arrive at VNE=300kts.

The AP1565J and L contain recommended minimum entry speeds for aerobatic manoeuvres and the following limitations shall apply:
Aerobatic limitations – Aerobatics are permitted in accordance with the pilot's notes.
Intentional spinning is prohibited.

Loading limitations

The maximum take-off weight authorised is 7,500lb.
The maximum landing weight authorised is 7,500lb.
The CoG range is 3½in aft of datum to 7in aft of datum.

Engine limitations

Start-up	Max rpm 1,000; coolant temp min 40°C; oil temp min 15°C.
Take-off	Max rpm 3,000; Boost +12; coolant min 60°C, max 135°C; oil temp min 15°C, max 90°C.
Climb	Max rpm 2,850; boost +9; coolant max 125°C; oil temp max 90°C.
Max cruise	Min rpm 1,800, max rpm 2,650; boost +7; coolant temp max 105°C; oil temp max 90°C.

Airspeed limitations

VNE (Velocity Never Exceed) 300kts.
Undercarriage and flaps lowering, VNE 140kts.

Other limitations

The aircraft shall be flown for VMC (Visual Meteorological Conditions) over land or water between sea level and 10,000ft.

The aircraft may be operated from tarmac, concrete and prepared grass runways.
Operations in conditions of snow, ice, slush or freezing rain are prohibited.

Conditions affecting airworthiness

The applicant has provided a statement that all applicable MPDs (Mandatory Permit Directives) and ADs (Airworthiness Directives) have been complied with. The influence of MPD eligibility and other data must be considered and the publications monitored accordingly. The maintenance schedule of the aircraft should include reference to the material additional to the original design.

Survey

The aircraft G-BBMF has been surveyed by the CAA; in particular, all areas examined during the survey of the aircraft were found to conform with the standard recorded by this ANN.

Issue of permit to fly

The following actions must be completed prior to the official issue of the permit to fly.
All actions and ground-test procedures specified by the aircraft manufacturer must be completed satisfactorily.

It must be verified that the documents or amendments to document, and the placards defined above, are as specified, including any changes mentioned by the CAA, found during the survey.

The aircraft has been flight tested by Bill Smith, who has been accepted by the CAA, to flight test schedule 01. The flight test schedule report 01 dated 31/03/2008 and email from Bill Smith on 4/04/2008 confirm that the aircraft is acceptable for the issue of a permit to fly.

Approval

Subject to the conditions above, this aircraft is approved for the issue of a permit to fly, provided it is operated in accordance with the limitations specified/referenced that it confirms with the contents of this AAN.

Once your CAA inspector is happy with your paperwork and the standard of build, then your aircraft should be signed off and given a permit to fly! As part of getting your permit, the inspector will also need to see a plan of proposed maintenance and operating procedures. Your aircraft cannot fly until you have received all the paperwork from the CAA, and you will be issued with your permit to test. When that is successfully completed you will be issued with a permit to fly, which has to be renewed every year.

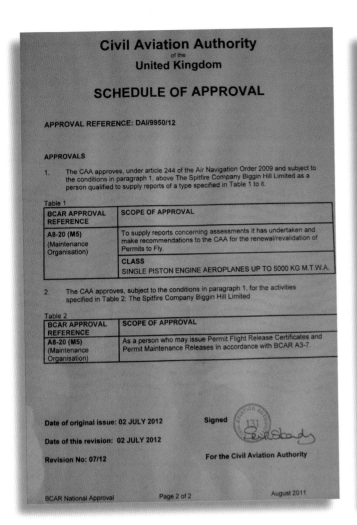

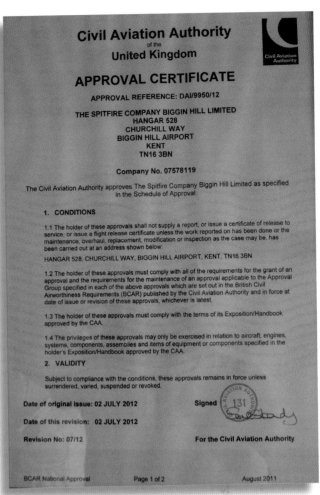

Flight testing

With the opportunity now in hand to fly your aircraft for the first time you should consider whether a full air test is the best course of action. Everything on the ground, when checked, worked correctly – for example, the undercarriage operated properly and the engine had been adjusted during its engine runs – so the temptation is to go for a full air test. However, it is probably more prudent to take a cautious approach and plan several short flights, to enable the pilot to get a feel for the aircraft and to make sure that it flies as it should, with no bad handling characteristics that would need addressing.

It is important to test things such as gear going up and down and ensuring that the system pipework, oil and coolant is coping with the actual pressure of flight. Any leaks are then able to be identified and sorted out. Once

you are happy that there are no major issues and everything seems to be doing what it is supposed to, and will hopefully stay that way, then it's time for the full air test.

This test is designed to confirm that the aircraft performs correctly under the stresses and strains of normal flight and display. The pilot will be given a schedule that he fills out during this flight, in order to ascertain that engine rpm, boost pressure, coolant and oil temperatures and pressure are all within limits. The flight test also checks out the stalling characteristics of the aircraft and also the engine performance in a climb to 7,000ft. This flight should last approximately 30 minutes if everything goes well.

On completion of the test the pilot should debrief the team as to whether any adjustments are required to the engine and whether there are any defects that need rectifying on the aircraft.

ABOVE LEFT CAA Schedule of Approval A8-20 (M5), issued to The Spitfire Company/ Biggin Hill Heritage Hangar. *(Paul Blackah)*

ABOVE The conditions of the Approval. *(Paul Blackah)*

Once an aircraft has completed ground runs, passed the CAA inspections etc, it is ready for the first air test – a time of great anticipation for both the pilot and also the restoration team. This will be the moment that defines the work that has taken place over the last few months/years, and also the future work should there be any 'snags' identified during the air test.

Squadron Leader Ian Smith, currently OC RAF BBMF, takes us through an air test similar to the one that would be performed on a restored to airworthy Spitfire project:

As OC RAF BBMF I am often asked how I feel about working with and caring for the historic aircraft on the Flight, especially the Spitfire. The closest analogy I can come to is that of owning an old classic car: too valuable to drive over the winter and so in that time you put it into the workshops for a deep servicing. Expert technicians then dismantle it, carefully cataloguing parts and send various bits and pieces off to subject matter experts to be reconditioned or serviced. It's not that the workshop [personnel] don't have the skill sets to do everything but it is more cost effective to employ experts in their fields to recondition items such as engines and radiators.

Over the winter the car is stripped to its bare chassis and while all the main components are away it is inspected, repaired where necessary, and then put to one side. All its major components are sent away and their condition will decide what the course of action is. Wear or damage or even age will define whether that part is just serviced, overhauled or reconditioned.

Early in the New Year parts start arriving back at the workshops and at this point they can be refitted to the car. Once a system is complete it can be statically tested, although there is an element of chicken and egg here, as some systems require virtually all others to be complete before they can function correctly.

Once it is all back together it will visit the paint shop for a touch-up and then it is ready for a test drive!

It is exactly the same scenario for a Spitfire having been through winter maintenance; the only difference is that a Spitfire cannot be pulled into the side of the road on its test drive if something goes wrong!

I have ultimate faith in my engineers who have carried out the winter maintenance schedule. They are masters in their art and, although an aircraft that is likely 70 years old is always quirky, I have no doubt that it will behave itself in most if not all respects.

There is a laid-down air-test schedule to which I will adhere. By doing so I will ensure that everything is covered and we can look back at previous results and compare them.

The weather has to be excellent. We are not allowed to fly in cloud or rain and there are enough pressures on an air test without having to worry about the weather. The wind needs to be benign as well, as most of these old warbird types have very limited crosswind limits.

The engineers will have statically tested the engine, but as I start it for the air test I am very interested to see that it remains within its temperature and pressure limits. Any leaks at this stage will be obvious to the see-off ground crew and all being well I will taxy towards the runway. The brakes are likely to be poor as there are new pads inside new drums and, despite being 'scuffed' before they were fitted, they will take time to bed in.

Ready for take-off and despite my faith in the team up to this point my heart is racing as any problems from this point onwards are going to

BELOW The walk-round checks are carried out before each flight. Here, Squadron Leader Ian Smith is checking the rudder and elevator for any restrictions in movement. *(Karl Bacon)*

LEFT Making sure the spinner is secure.
(Karl Bacon)

be complicated! I can't simply pull over to the side of the road in the event of an engine failure!

All one's senses are highly tuned at this point: eyes scan the instruments, ears listen for normal noises, but, more importantly, strange noises, and nose and eyes are starboard side. On the BBMF Mark XIX Spitfires an extra six weights, weighing 17½lb each, are installed in these positions. These weights are there because the camera assemblies are not fitted to the aircraft.

I'm tuned into strange smells or fumes.

Often you can smell trouble before it happens and stinging eyes is a sure sign of fumes and trouble ahead.

The engine pulls strongly at take-off power and with temperatures, pressures and engine revving all within limits I commit to take off rather than abort and lift her off the ground. A satisfying thump is felt as the wheels lock into their wells and I reduce engine revs and boost to climb power. The climb to 7,000ft is timed to assess performance and while still highly anxious I am at least more comfortable that

LEFT Getting strapped in prior to the start.
(Crown Copyright/RAF Coningsby)

ABOVE Squadron Leader Ian Smith about to start the engine. *(Karl Bacon)*

height along with a check of flight instruments, compass, GPS and fuel usage.

Once settled at 7,000ft, the engine gets a breather as it is back at cruise power as I set the aircraft up for a stall, both clean and then with undercarriage and flaps lowered. This test ensures that the aircraft behaves predictably, especially if the flying controls have been disturbed during maintenance. It also allows me to time both undercarriage and flap extension and retraction, all of which must be within predefined limits. Always very satisfying to feel the wheels lock down the first time and to know that the system is serviceable!

Next is a series of engine checks at various revs and boost settings. Parameters and performance are noted at each setting, which will be assessed once back on the ground. My confidence in my mount is now growing as I have proven that all the systems are working normally and I can even relax just about enough to start enjoying the experience.

Next event is a high-speed dive down to 2,000ft, which proves the airframe handling at

all seems well and that the aircraft is behaving itself. I remain relatively close to base as it's wise never to get too far away from the airfield in case of having to get on the ground quickly. Engine parameters are recorded in the climb to

RIGHT TE311's first flight since 1954. *(Keith Wilson)*

high speeds, but also checks the Automatic
Boost Control in the engine on the way down.
Once complete the air test is effectively
complete, but I increase engine rpm and boost
to display settings and then carry out a series
of aerobatic manoeuvres to check handling
and performance. Typically I will try and do this
over the airfield because the ground crew will
undoubtedly be watching and this aerial ballet
will signify to them that all is going well. They
are equally apprehensive during an air test as
it is their signatures against the multitude of
tasks that they carried out over the winter. Who
wouldn't want to watch a Spitfire cavorting
around the skies anyway?

Final act is to 'beat up' the hangar as I
position the aircraft in the circuit to land. That is
my way of telling the boys that it has passed its
air test before even having seen them!

Wheels and flap down I fly the classic curved
Spitfire approach and gently flare her on to the
ground. Twenty-five minutes goes extremely
quickly when you are busy!

Safely back on the chocks and the boys all
gather around, keen to see how she behaved.
Bar a few minor tweaks she is in rude health

and smiles break out among the gathering.

It is some engineering achievement to have
a 70-plus-year-old aeroplane in so many pieces
over a six-month period and then have her all
back together again and ready to fly and they
are justifiably proud of their achievements.

My job as air-test pilot is complete. No need
to coast to the side of the road and peer under
the bonnet.

On 19 October 2012, Squadron Leader Ian
Smith had the privilege of being the first person
to fly Spitfire TE311 for over 58 years. Initially
all went well and a round of applause went up
as her wheels left the ground and she took to
the air. However, as he proceeded around the
circuit it became evident to onlookers that the
aircraft had not retracted the undercarriage and
so he came straight in to land again.

It seemed that the undercarriage would
not retract and therefore the air test could not
be carried out. He was thrilled, though, with
the initial handling of the aircraft. It was to be
another two weeks before the air test was
carried out, during which time the ground crew
corrected the problem and TE311 went on to

RIGHT After a
successful flight, the
team get to celebrate
their achievement. Left
to right: Ben Robinson,
Jim Douthwaite, Paul
Blackah, 'Sticky' Bunn
and Andy Bale.
(Karl Bacon)

complete her air test with flying colours. She is
a great addition to the team, performing at air
shows around the country.

Maintenance

Your aircraft has flown, passed its air test
and will now be regularly flown. At this
stage you have to consider what maintenance
schedule you will set in place and follow. This
will depend on how often you plan to fly your
aircraft; in other words, how many hours you
intend to fly in a given period, such as a year.

It is possible to ask other operators for
advice as to their maintenance schedules; at
BBMF it is not uncommon for private operators
to contact the Flight and ask for a copy of the
maintenance schedules, so that they can base
their own around an already proven system. For
the purpose of this book, we will take a brief
look at the BBMF's scheduling, which is used
by private operators also.

Pre-flight maintenance

The engineer will examine the aircraft to ensure
that all the panels are secure, and observe the
general condition of the aircraft to make certain
no skins are cracking and no leaks are evident,
that tyre pressures are appropriate, the oleos
are checked for the correct extension, fuel
tanks are full and the oil and coolant levels are
where they should be.

Electrical power is switched on to make sure
of the right battery voltage and that nav lights
are working; undercarriage indication is also

inspected for the two greens showing, indicating
undercarriage lock-down. The pitot heater is
turned on to confirm that it heats up, the flying
controls are moved through their ranges to
ensure there are no restrictions, the windscreen
is cleaned and the parachute is checked to see
that the red cotton safety is intact. The aircraft is
then signed up as ready for flight.

After-flight maintenance

The pilot hands the aircraft back to the ground
crew and it is then refuelled. The windscreen
is washed to remove dead flies, and a general
look over the airframe, as above, is carried
out and the aircraft cleaned to remove any oil
streaks and flies.

Primary servicing (mid-season)

This is generally carried out after 28 hours of
flight. It is not terribly in-depth and if you are not
planning to fly this amount of hours per year,
you could do this earlier.

It is, basically, a look over of the aircraft,
checking for wear and tear. A clean of the oil
and water trap to remove any oil is done and
the engine filters checked for any debris. The
magneto contact breaker points are inspected
to make sure they have the correct gaps, and
the aircraft is lubricated at flying control hinge
points and undercarriage. Once completed an
engine ground run is carried out to examine
for leaks around the filter assemblies and the
aircraft is then ready to go again.

This servicing should take one or two people
approximately one or two days.

Annual servicing

This service is undertaken annually and could be done within two months with two or three people dedicated to the task; obviously longer with fewer personnel. On the BBMF, the aircraft have generally flown for approximately 70 hours prior to their annual servicing; however, even if the hours are significantly less, the service is still carried out on an annual basis.

The aircraft is put on jacks and is de-panelled for inspection. The undercarriage legs are removed, as are the undercarriage locking mechanism eye bolts. The eye bolts and the undercarriage pintles are checked for cracking using NDT techniques. The airframe is looked over for damage, cracking, corrosion or loose rivets and rectified if anything is found.

Flying control cables are monitored for fraying and general wear and tear. The hydraulic, oil and coolant pipes are inspected for leaks and damage to the pipework. Any damaged pipes are replaced; most damage to pipework is caused by chafing against framework or other pipes. Replacement pipes would need to be manufactured using a company such as Supermarine Engineering.

The engine cam assemblies are examined for wear on the cam lobes and rocker arms and the engine flame traps are cleaned. Again, the filters are checked and the engine oil is changed. A SOAP (Spectromatic Oil Analysis Programme) sample is taken and sent away to investigate for any metal particles, which may suggest that the engine components, such as the bearings or piston rings, may be breaking down. If a high reading is returned it may mean that your engine will need a complete flush and oil change and a further SOAP taken after the next flight. If the reading after that flight remains high, then the engine would need to be removed for inspection by a specialist company.

The undercarriage oleos have their oil replaced and any component that requires bay maintenance; this would be an item that has a 'life' (so many hours' use or so many years installed), such as a propeller, which is 360 flying hours or 6 years, or an air bottle, which has a 5-year life.

On refit all the systems will need to have functional assessments; for example, the

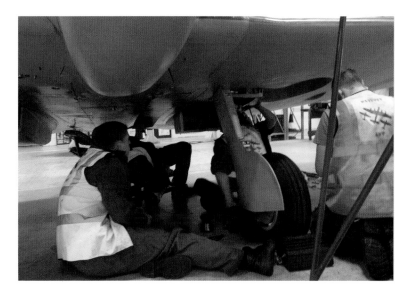

undercarriage retraction tests, flying control range of movements and ground running the engine. On completion of the servicing the aircraft is given a full air test.

The paperwork is then signed off and a permit is given for a further 12 months.

ABOVE Taking out panels to gain access to remove the radiator assembly. *(Paul Blackah)*

And finally...

The last word should really go to co-author Paul Blackah on his feelings as his 'baby' takes to the skies, restoration complete:

As a restorer, nothing prepares you for that stomach-lurching feeling as the wheels lift off the ground for the first time and you hold your breath hoping that everything goes well, stays in place and simply works! TE311 had a few snags when she first began to fly; however, despite trying my patience for a few weeks, we soon resolved those initial problems and she joined the RAF BBMF's fleet, working the 2013 air show season.

Despite not flying her myself, the enormous thrill that I have when I see her in the air, hear the comments from those who watch her alongside those who are flying her, gives me a huge sense of pride and achievement. Yes, there may be a few more grey hairs, many more if truth be known, after the last few years of pulling everything together, but once TE311's wheels leave the tarmac, the undercarriage raises and she begins to display then I know that it's all been worthwhile. Would I do it again? Well ... who knows?!

Appendices

Appendix 1 –

Some of the aircraft under restoration in 2013

Appendix 2 –

Useful addresses and sources of information

OPPOSITE Spitfire Mark IX (TD314) nears completion at Biggin Hill and is expected to fly again in 2014. *(Paul Blackah)*

Some of the aircraft under restoration in 2013

RW382 Spitfire Mark XVI
(Spitfire LF Mark XVIe (CBAF IX 4640) G-PBIX (1945))

1945

Built in 1945 and delivered from Castle Bromwich to No 6 MU at Brize Norton on 20 July.

1947–50

No 604 Squadron RAuxAF on 1 April 1947, serving until 14 April 1950, when it was retired to No 33 MU, Lyneham.

1950–53

Joined No 3 Civilian Anti-Aircraft Co-operation Unit at Exeter on 11 June 1950, transferring to the Control and Reporting School at Middle Wallop on 17 October of that year.

1953

BELOW RW382's first flight is imminent.

Final retirement came on 14 July 1953, when it flew to No 45 MU at Kinloss, moving on to No 29 MU at High Ercall two weeks later. SOC on 14 December 1954.

28 November 1955

Allocated to No 609 Squadron at Church Fenton as instructional airframe 7245M (although it was painted as M7245 at some time).

1957–73

RAF gate guard at Leconfield as RW729/DW-X.

1967–68

At Henlow, RAF. Used in the film *Battle of Britain* for static scenes, 1968.

1973–88

RAF, displayed on a pole in Uxbridge.

1988–89

Tim Routsis/Historic Flying Ltd, Cambridge.

1989–91

David Tallichet/MARC, Chino, CA.

1991

Tim Routsis/Historic Flying Ltd at Audley End, registered as G-XVIA.

3 July 1991

First flight as RW382/NG-C at Audley End.

1991–94

Military Aircraft Restoration Corp, Chino, CA.

1994–95

Bernie F. Jackson, Manitoba, Canada.

1991–95

Based in UK.

13 February 1995

Arrived at Audley End to be dismantled for shipment to USA.

1995–98

F. Thomas and Bernie Jackson, Blenbrook, NV. Registered as N382RW.

3 June 1998

Crashed in mountain canyon, Blue Canyon, CA. Registered as G-PBIX by Pemberton-Billing LLP.

2011

Restoration to fly at the Spitfire Company (Biggin Hill) Ltd.

TD314 Spitfire Mark IX
(Spitfire HF Mark IXe (CBAF IX 10492) G-CGYJ (1944))

ABOVE TD314 well on the way to completion at Biggin Hill.

1944
Built at CBAF in 1944 with a Merlin 70 fitted.
1945
Delivered to 33 MU at Lyneham on 30 March 1945. Delivered to 183 (Gold Coast) Squadron at Chilbolton on 24 June 1945. Delivered to 234 (Madras Presidency) Squadron at Bentwaters on 26 July 1945.
27 February 1946
Delivered to 29 MU at High Ercall for disposal.
23 April 1948
Sent to 47 MU RAF Sealand, packed for shipment, leaving Birkenhead on the SS *Clan Chattan*, arriving Cape Town 12 May 1948.
1948
Delivered to SAAF.

1954
South African Metal & Machinery Co., Salt River, Cape Town.
1969–72
Larry Barnet, Johannesburg, recovered hulk.
1978–81
Pat Swonnell, Vancouver, BC. Fuselage arrived by ship, 11 April 1979.
1985
Matt Sattler, Carp, Ontario.
2009
To Peter Monk Ltd, UK, for restoration.
2011
Registered to Keith Perkins.
2011
Under restoration to fly at the Spitfire Company (Biggin Hill) Ltd.

TE517 Spitfire LF Mark IXe
(Spitfire LF Mark IXe (CBAF IX 558) G-JGCA (1945))

1945
Delivered to RAF as TE517.

June 1945
Accepted by 33 MU, allocated to 313 Squadron.

1945–48
Delivered to the Czech Air Force as TE517. BOC 20 August 1945. SOC 1948.

1948–54
Delivered to Israeli Defence Force AF as 20-46. BOC 1948. SOC 1954.

1977–84
Robs Lamplough, Duxford. Hulk recovered from kibbutz at Gaaton, Israel. Registration G-BIXP, 3 July 1981. Restoration commenced at Bristol.

1985–92
Charles Church (Spitfires) Ltd, Winchester. Registered as G-CCIX.

1992–2002
Kermit A. Weeks, Tamiami, FL.

2002–12
Private storage.

2012
Under restoration by The Spitfire Company (Biggin Hill) Ltd at the Biggin Hill Heritage Hangar, Biggin Hill.

Also on long-term restoration at Biggin Hill are Spitfires Mark IX, LZ842, Mark V, EP122 and Mark XVI, TB885.

RIGHT LZ842's fuselage in desert camouflage.

BELOW LZ842 is the next in line for rebuild at the Biggin Hill Heritage Hangar.

BELOW RIGHT TE517 is another Spitfire waiting to be rebuilt to flying condition at Biggin Hill.

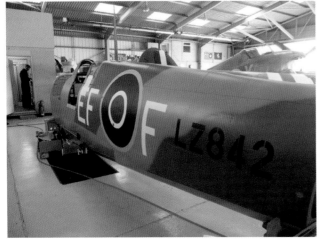

At the Aircraft Restoration Company (Arco) is Spitfire MarkV, AB910. This aircraft has been included because although it is there on a major servicing, this is going to take approximately two years. She has been completely stripped down and is going to have new wing spars and quite a few of her fuselage skins replaced, and removal of repairs that were carried out after her taxiing accident in Switzerland in the 1970s.

HISTORY OF AB910	
1941	Built at Castle Bromwich.
1941, August	Assigned to 222 Squadron.
1941	Assigned to 130 Squadron.
1942, June	Delivered to 133 Eagle Squadron, involved in raid on Dieppe. Flew operationally up to July 1944 with 242, 416 and 402 RCAF Squadrons. From mid-July 1944 flew with 53 OTU and later with 527 Squadron.
Post-war	Flew as an air racer for six years.
1953	Refurbished by Vickers-Armstrongs where she was flown by Jeffrey Quill.
1965	Donated to RAF BBMF.
1978	Accident in Switzerland and rebuilt using a Mark IX for spares.
2012	To Arco, Duxford, for major refurbishment.

BELOW AB910's wing spars in the jig at Arco, Duxford.

ABOVE Fuselage skins removed to examine the frames/intercostals and longerons.

LEFT AB910's frame 5 partially stripped.

Useful addresses and sources of information

Aerospace Support International
21B Monument Business Park,
Chalgrove,
Oxford, OX44 7RW.
Tel: 01865 400106
Email: sales@aerospaceintl.com
Aircraft general spares using worldwide search.

Airframe Assemblies
Hangar 6S,
Isle of Wight airport,
Sandown,
Isle of Wight, PO36 OJP.
Tel: 01983 408661/404462
Produces replacement airframes.

Air Historical Branch (RAF)
Building 824,
RAF Northolt,
West End Road,
Ruislip,
Middlesex HA4 6NG.
Tel: 02088 338175
Email: ahb.raf@btconnect.com
Hold records and movement cards of aircraft.

Anglia Radiators
Unit 4,
Stanley Road,
Cambridge, CB5 8LB.
Tel: 01223 314444
Builds replacement radiators and oil coolers.

ARCO
Duxford airfield,
Cambridgeshire,
CB2 4QR.
Tel: 01223 835313
Provides maintenance facilities for historic
aircraft.

Bruntons Aero Products Ltd
Units 1–3, Block 1, Inveresk Industrial Estate,
Musselburgh, East Lothian,
Scotland,
EH21 7PA.
Tel: 0131 665 3888
Email: www.bruntons.co.uk
Flying control cables.

Butser Rubber Ltd
Mint Road,
Liss,
Hampshire, GU33 7BQ.
Tel: 01730 894034
Email: sales@butserrubber.com
Rubber seals.

Civil Aviation Authority
Aviation House,
Gatwick Airport South,
West Sussex, RH6 0YR.
Tel: 01293 567171
Applications and approvals (certificates of air
worthiness and permit to fly).

Dowty Propellers
Anson Business Park,
Cheltenham Road East,
Gloucester,
GL2 9QN.
Tel: 01452 716000
Builds and refurbishes propellers.

Dunlop Tyres
40 Fort Parkway,
Erdington,
Birmingham,
West Midlands,
B24 9HL.
Produces replacement tyres for Spitfires.

Hanley Smith
7 South Road,
Templefields, Harlow,
Essex, CM20 2AP.
Tel: 01279 414446
Overhauls undercarriage legs.

Historic Flying
Duxford airfield,
Cambridgeshire, CB2 4QR.
Tel: 01223 839455
Builds and restores Spitfires.

Personal Plane Services Ltd
Wycombe Air Park, Booker Marlow,
Buckinghamshire, SL7 3DS.
Tel: 01494 449810
Overhauls and rebuilds aircraft.

RAF Hendon Aircraft Museum
Royal Air Force Museum London,
Grahame Park Way,
London, NW9 5LL.
Tel: 02082 052266
Email: London@rafmuseum.org
Has copies of aircraft drawings and manuals.

Retro Track and Air
Upthorpe Iron Works,
Upthorpe Lane,
Dursley,
Gloucestershire, GL11 5HP.
Overhauls engines, engine components and airframe components.

Skycraft
12 Silver Street,
Litlington,
Nr Royston,
Hertfordshire, SG8 0QE.
Builds and refurbishes propellers.

Smiths Industries, Aerospace
www.smiths-aerospace.com
Aircraft instruments.

The Spitfire Company/Biggin Hill Heritage Hangar Ltd
Website: www.bigginhillheritagehangar.co.uk
Email: admin@bigginhillheritagehangar.co.uk
Restores and operates Spitfires.

Supermarine Aero Engineering Ltd
Mitchell Works,
Steventon Place,
Burslem,
Stoke-on-Trent,
Stafford, ST6 4AS.
Tel: 01782 811344
Machine components.

Vintage Fabrics Ltd
Mitchell Hangar,
Audley End airfield,
Saffron Waldon,
Essex, CB11 4LH.
Tel: 01799 510756
Refabrics the flying controls and resprays aircraft.

VMI Engineering Services Ltd
9HTH Complex,
Blackwater Way,
Aldershot,
Hampshire, GU12 4DN.
Email : vmiengineering@live.co.uk
Restores Spitfire wings and fuselages.

Vokes Air
Farrington Road,
Burnley,
Lancashire, BB11 5SY
Tel: 01282 413131
Hydraulic and air filters.

Watts Aviation Services Ltd
Church Road,
Lydney,
Gloucestershire, GL15 5EN.
Tel: 01594 847290
Email: info@wattsaviation.co.uk
Tyres.

Books

Morgan, Eric and Shacklady, Edward. *Spitfire: The History* (2nd revised edition, Key Books, 2000).
Reference source for the general history, which includes the factory serial numbers and RAF squadron codes for the majority of Spitfires produced. This will enable you to find the serial number using your data plate.

Index